THE CHILDREN'S BREAD

LUKE BRUGGER
MINISTRIES

Learn more at
www.LukeBrugger.com

THE CHILDREN'S BREAD

DISCOVERING GOD'S WILL TO HEAL

LUKE BRUGGER

Book design by eBook Prep
www.ebookprep.com

October 2023
ISBN: 978-1-64457-642-7 (Paperback)
ISBN: 978-1-64457-646-5 (Hardcover)

Rise UP Publications
644 Shrewsbury Commons Ave
Ste 249
Shrewsbury PA 17361
United States of America

www.riseUPpublications.com
Phone: 866-846-5123

CONTENTS

Foreword   13

Introduction   15

CHAPTER 1   17
Jesus Is Passionate About Your Healing

Do Not Be Passive   22

CHAPTER 2   27
Spiritual Roots to Sickness

God Is Pleased by Your Request   31

Understanding the Level of Bread   33

Healing = the Children's Bread   34

Healing Comes by Faith   37

The Provision has Been Made   39

CHAPTER 3   41
Unlimited Supply

2 Keys the Gentile Woman Grasped   46

CHAPTER 4   51
Make Sure You Have What is Yours

What Does it Mean to Walk By Faith?   56

CHAPTER 5   61
The Word Precedes Healing

The Word As Bread For Healing   63

God's Word as Medicine   65

What is the prescription/directions?   66

Beth's Testimony   75

The Word Precedes Healing   77

God's Word is a Sword   82

CHAPTER 6   85
Base Level Provision

Provision Has Been Made   87

CHAPTER 7   97
Healing in Communion
Why Bother with the Bread?   101
Healing in the 23rd Psalm   109

CHAPTER 8   113
The Father's Provision on Display
Healing is the Showbread   117
The Spiritual Impacting the Natural   120

CHAPTER 9   133
Use It

Afterword   139
Healing Confessions Based on Scripture   141
About the Author   145

Dedicated to my mom & dad, Dianne & Gene Brugger.

Thank you for raising me to know Jesus. Thank you for loving me unconditionally. Thank you for the example you have given me to follow. Thank you for living sacrificially so I could go further.

May I never forget the good things He does for me. He forgives all my sins and heals all my diseases.

— KING DAVID

FOREWORD

Pastor Luke possesses a rare gift: the ability to take profound truths from the Word of God and present them in a simple and accessible manner. Throughout my 15 years of ministry, I have witnessed the unfortunate trend toward over-complicating the message of healing. Consequently, many of our brothers and sisters in Christ find themselves trapped in a state of frustration and fear over sickness and disease. As Hosea 4:6 reminds us, "My people are destroyed for lack of knowledge." It is imperative that we grasp the understanding of what already belongs to us in order to walk in divine health.

The pages of this book illuminate the straightforward and attainable truth concerning your healing. Healing is our inheritance as children of God—a foundational provision akin to a basket of bread served before a sumptuous steak dinner at a restaurant! Just as this book served as a catalyst for my journey toward health and healing, it has the power to ignite the same transformative process in your life, day after day.

Adalis Shuttlesworth, Pastor

INTRODUCTION

At the Church, where I pastor, whenever we do a series that focuses on relationships, we begin nearly every service with a few basic ground rules. We do this because of the sensitive nature of relationships and because so many mistakes have already been made in some people's lives.

When we talk about what God's Word says regarding strong, healthy relationships, some people realize their mistakes and recognize the pain those mistakes have caused. Others realize things could have been so different if they had lived according to God's Word. The enemy will try to make people feel condemned and ashamed.

One ground rule we establish is that whatever mistakes you have made in your past are in your past. What has already happened has already happened. There is no condemnation for those who are in Christ Jesus. We will take the truth we are learning and, rather than use it to feel bad about our past, choose to walk in it moving forward.

Talking about healing can be similar. Maybe a family member, a friend, or you personally, have wrestled with health issues. As we look at God's

Word and see His provision for healing, the enemy tries to bring discouragement and condemnation on some.

As you receive new revelation, the Devil wants to twist it into something that will weigh you down instead of lift you up. He wants you bound with condemnation, not experiencing the freedom God desires. I want to apply the same ground rule here. Maybe you have missed it in the area of healing in your past. Perhaps you completely misunderstood what the Bible says about healing. What is in the past is in the past. We will take the Word of God, and from this point forward, we will apply it to our lives.

The Bible tells us God's Word is light. When light comes, it removes all darkness. Light doesn't remove some darkness and replace it with a different kind of darkness. When the light of God's Word reveals something new, it is to free us from whatever darkness was in our lives. God gives revelation concerning healing to free us from the burden of sickness, not to replace it with a yoke of regret.

Light comes to set us free from lies and confusion. If you realize you have been wrong, be thankful for new understanding. Don't allow condemnation to make you feel bad for mistakes made in the past.

Let God speak to you and bring fresh revelation about what a wonderful Father He is. If divine health and healing haven't been real in your life until now, don't feel bad about it. Instead, determine it will become your reality moving forward.

CHAPTER 1

JESUS IS PASSIONATE ABOUT YOUR HEALING

Let all that I am praise the Lord; may I never forget the
good things he does for me. He forgives all my sins
and heals all my diseases.

— PSALM 103:2, 3 (NLT)

One of the greatest benefits of serving God is walking in perfect
health. In Psalm 103, King David begins to list the benefits.
While some might argue that healing is not a benefit at all or may try to
lessen its importance, David places it second only to the forgiveness of
sins.

Unfortunately, many of God's children are missing out on this
wonderful benefit. While there are many reasons why Christians go
without the health and healing that belongs to them, one of the
primary reasons is they are simply unsure of God's desire to heal them.

When we desire to know something about the will of God, a great
place to start is by observing the life of Jesus. In the book of Hebrews,
we are told that the life of Jesus is one of the fundamental ways God
speaks to us today.

> Long ago God spoke many times and in many ways to
> our ancestors through the prophets. And now in
> these final days, he has spoken to us through
> His Son.
>
> — HEBREWS 1:1, 2A (NLT)

Jesus said He came to carry out the will of the Father (John 6:38). He also said that when you see Him, you see the Father (John 14:9). Reading through the Gospels and observing the life of Jesus is an excellent way to understand the heart of the Father. Matthew, Mark, Luke, and John allow us to learn about the things Jesus did while here on earth. We can read about the things He said and some of the things He taught. We can read about how He treated people and how He responded to various situations.

While studying the life of Jesus, one story stands out because it doesn't seem to fit with the other things Jesus did. Reading through the Gospels, you read of Jesus showing love and being kind. He is forgiving, gracious, and gentle. He feeds hungry people. He holds children on his lap. He touches lepers and loves the outcast.

Then, in John chapter 2, we encounter what seems to be another side of Jesus. This is key because it reveals something significant about God's attitude toward sickness and disease.

> Now the Passover of the Jews was at hand, and Jesus went
> up to Jerusalem. And He found in the temple those
> who sold oxen and sheep and doves, and the money
> changers doing business. When He had made a whip
> of cords, He drove them all out of the temple, with
> the sheep and the oxen, and poured out the changers'
> money and overturned the tables. And He said to

those who sold doves, "Take these things away! Do not make My Father's house a house of merchandise!" Then His disciples remembered that it was written, "Zeal for Your house has eaten Me up."

— JOHN 2:13-17 (NKJV)

When people are upset or angry, there are a variety of ways they can express themselves. Some people become quiet and don't want to talk. When others are angry, they get loud and want to yell. Some people get emotional and cry. Others stomp their feet. If someone is very upset, they may throw something or punch a wall.

Think about when you felt the most intense anger you have ever felt. Chances are, as upset as you were, you didn't destroy furniture in a public place or chase an entire crowd away with a weapon.

In the above passage from John 2, Jesus visits the temple, and what He finds there angers Him intensely. He doesn't become cold and withdrawn. He doesn't vent his frustration to His disciples or have a good cry. He doesn't stomp His feet or punch a wall in response. His reaction is far more extreme. He made a whip and chased people with it. He dumped out people's money. He overturned their tables.

This isn't the way we think of Jesus. This is the conduct of an intolerant and violent man. What triggered this kind of behavior? What got Jesus so upset and furious that He flipped furniture over and caused people to run away in fear?

There were things in the temple that did not belong there. What was happening inside the temple was so unacceptable that Jesus took what can only be considered extreme action to fix the situation.

Jesus had a *violent* reaction when there were activities in the temple that didn't belong there. When conditions were out of order in the Temple, it moved Jesus to do whatever was necessary to correct it.

If simply asking the money changers to move along would have been effective, that is what Jesus would have done. If shooing them away with a motion of his hand or simply expressing that He didn't like them there would have worked, then that is what Jesus would have done. But because Jesus was consumed with a passion for God's dwelling place, He was willing to do whatever was necessary to restore proper order to the Temple. Restoring in the Temple required flipping furniture and chasing people with a whip, so that is exactly what Jesus did.

In the New Covenant, God's presence is no longer confined to a particular building. In this New Covenant, He dwells within those who have accepted Jesus as Savior. The Bible even calls our bodies the "Temple of the Holy Spirit."

> Or do you not know that your body is the temple of
> the Holy Spirit who is in you, whom you have
> from God, and you are not your own?
>
> — 1 CORINTHIANS 6:19 (NKJV)

When Jesus cleansed the Temple, He showed us God's desire to cleanse His children's bodies of sickness and disease. He gave us insight into how God feels toward illness in your body. He wants nothing in the temple that does not belong there.

To confirm this is exactly what was taking place, pay attention to Jesus' "temple cleansing technique." The method Jesus chose to cleanse the Temple in John 2 is the same means He used to secure healing for your body, a whip.

In John 2, when Jesus observed the condition of the Temple and the things happening there, He could have driven the people out any number of ways. He could have picked up a handful of rocks and thrown them at people. He could have used a stick or a limb from a tree. When He was tipping over the furniture, He could have broken a leg off a table or used one of the money changer's chairs to drive people away. We know from John 18:10 that Peter carried a sword. Jesus could have borrowed it. Jesus didn't do any of those things. Even though these other options would have been far more convenient, He was very intentional about using a whip.

Jesus specifically wanted to use a whip to remove what did not belong in the Temple. In fact, He was so insistent on using a whip that when one was not available, He made one Himself (John 2:15).

Jesus used a whip to remove what did not belong in the temple. When we read Isaiah 53, what we find in verses 4-5, parallels Jesus' cleansing of the Temple in John 2.

Jesus died on the cross so we could be forgiven of our sins and be saved. But before He was nailed to the cross, the Bible says Jesus was beaten with a whip (Mark 15:15, John 19:1, Luke 23:16, Matthew 27:26). This beating with a whip left His body "striped" with wounds. Isaiah 53:5 tells us it is by those stripes we are healed. Just like a whip was used to cleanse the Temple, it was also a whip that provided cleansing for your body.

As Jesus' stunned disciples watched Him wield His handcrafted whip at the Temple that day, the Holy Spirit quickened a passage of scripture to them.

> Then his disciples remembered this prophecy from the
> Scriptures: "Passion for God's house will consume
> me."
>
> — JOHN 2:17 (NLT)

We know Jesus loves the Father. He directly stated His love in places like John 14:31. He also showed His love for the Father by His obedience, even to death on the cross. Passion for the Father is not what is mentioned here. What is mentioned is a specific passion that Jesus has for the physical dwelling place of God's presence.

Again, in the Old Testament, that dwelling place was the Temple in Jerusalem. In the New Covenant, it is the physical body of the believer that "houses" the presence of God.

Many believers think Jesus is unconcerned with physical things; they think if it is not spiritual, God does not regard it as important. Some consider attention given to our physical well-being as shallow. Not only does Jesus care, He is *consumed* with zeal for the "housing" of God's presence. Passion for God's house, His dwelling place, consumes Jesus!

Jesus was passionate about cleansing the Temple. As stated before, He was willing to do whatever was necessary to set things in order. He is just as passionate to see your body made whole and He has already done everything necessary to provide that wholeness.

Do Not Be Passive

In John 2, Jesus did not have a passive attitude toward things that did not belong in the Temple. To be like Jesus, we must have the same violent, intolerant attitude towards sickness. Provision has been made for our bodies to be healthy, but we must affirm that provision. Asserting your healing is the same as claiming your salvation. Salvation and forgiveness of sins have been made available for everyone. Romans 10:13 says, "For everyone who calls on the name of the Lord will be saved." Not everyone has been saved. Only those who profess by faith what God has provided, in His grace, *experience* that provision. It works the same way with healing. Just because it is available, doesn't mean you are walking in it.

In Acts 22, Roman soldiers took the Apostle Paul into custody. They bound him and were preparing to beat him. Right before the beating began, Paul spoke up. In Acts 22:25, Paul asked the soldiers, "Is it legal for you to whip a Roman citizen who hasn't even been tried?"

Paul's rights as a Roman citizen protected him from being beaten without a trial. Even though those rights were provided to him, something was still required of him. He had to actively claim those rights. What if Paul had just thought to himself, "Well, if the Romans don't want one of their citizens unfairly beaten, then I won't be beaten" or, "Looks like they've got the whip ready; I guess I don't really have the rights I thought I had." If Paul had remained silent, he would have taken the beating of a lifetime. Being passive about his rights was equivalent to forfeiting his rights.

It is the same with Christians and healing. There are very real benefits to being a citizen of the Kingdom of God, but just like Paul's Roman citizenship, you must speak up and lay claim to those benefits. Too many believers fall into the trap of being lazy and passive with their faith. When they feel symptoms of sickness coming on or receive a negative report from the doctor, they think, "Well, if God really wants me healthy, I'll be healthy. I guess healing isn't for everyone after all." That attitude would have gotten Paul beaten, and it will get you beaten as well.

Jesus would not have successfully cleared out the Temple with a calm, passive attitude; it required a weapon and a hostility toward what did not belong. When sickness tries to come on you, get violent and wield the weapon of the Word (Eph 6:17, 2 Co 10:4). The Bible says that by Jesus' stripes you were healed! Use that truth to violently drive sickness far from your body and your household. You must speak up to assert your rights.

Being passive is a choice to forfeit what belongs to you as a Child of God.

One of the things keeping people from claiming their healing with boldness is a lack of confidence that God truly desires them to be well. Being unsure of God's willingness to heal will keep you from having the faith necessary to receive.

> Now a leper came to Him, imploring Him, kneeling down to Him and saying to Him, "If You are willing, You can make me clean."
>
> — MARK 1:40 (NKJV)

This leper came to Jesus with confidence in Jesus' ability to heal. He knew Jesus *could* heal. The question in his mind was, "Is Jesus *willing* to heal?" He was like so many Christians today. Most believe that God can heal. In fact, they believe God can do anything. They are certain that nothing is impossible for God. Faith in God's ability is good, but it is not enough. You must also have faith in His love and His goodness. Bible faith is not only believing that God *can*; it is believing He *will*. Notice the progression of this next verse.

> Then Jesus, moved with compassion, stretched out His hand and touched him, and said to him, "I am willing; be cleansed."
>
> — MARK 1:41 (NKJV)

If Jesus had just healed this man, all questions about His willingness would have clearly been answered. A quick "Be healed!" would have been more dramatic. Before Jesus healed the man, something needed to be done. He could not go any further until this man moved from partial faith to complete faith. Jesus touched the man (which was against the law since he was a leper), looked at him, and told him, "I am willing."

Until the leper became confident in Jesus' willingness, Jesus couldn't heal him. His willingness had to be established first. This is Bible faith; not just knowing that God can, but knowing He wants to.

Hebrews 11:6 says those who come to God must do two things. They must "believe He exists" AND believe "He is a rewarder of those who seek Him."

There are two crucial aspects of Bible faith. Believing in God, believing He exists and is powerful and able to do the impossible is only *a part*. We must also believe He is a rewarder; He is a good, loving, merciful God who desires to bless His children. When you lack confidence in His goodness, you lack complete Bible faith.

Many people grow frustrated seeking healing from God, thinking that they are meeting the requirements of faith. They say things like, "I don't understand why I am not healed. I *KNOW* God can heal me. I fully believe God can do *anything*." They are like the leper in Mark 1 who needed to have God's willingness established before he could receive what God wanted him to have all along. To have Bible faith, we must not only believe God can, but also believe it is His desire.

God can heal you. God desires to heal you. God has already laid every sickness and disease on His son Jesus. By Jesus' stripes, the Bible says, healing is yours.

Do not be passive about it. Take a violent attitude. You *must* have what belongs to you.

Anything trying to occupy God's dwelling place that doesn't belong must be driven out by Jesus' stripes! Jesus was extremely passionate about there not being anything in the Temple that did not belong there. He used a whip to remove them.

By the stripes of Jesus, let every tumor, every virus, every germ of sickness, every disease, everything that does not belong, be driven far from your body today in Jesus' name!

Jesus clearly desired things to be in proper order in the Temple and used a whip to set them in order. He also desires everything in your body to be set in order. Everything that is out of order, every eyeball, every ear, every organ not functioning the way God designed it to function, must come back into proper order in Jesus' name.

In the following pages, you will see how your heavenly Father has already provided for your health and healing and how He wants you to enjoy His provision.

CHAPTER 2
SPIRITUAL ROOTS TO SICKNESS

Then Jesus went out from there and departed to the
region of Tyre and Sidon. And behold, a woman of
Canaan came from that region and cried out to
Him, saying, "Have mercy on me, O Lord, Son of
David! My daughter is severely demon-possessed."
But He answered her not a word. And His disciples
came and urged Him, saying, "Send her away, for
she cries out after us." But He answered and said,
"I was not sent except to the lost sheep of the house
of Israel." Then she came and worshiped Him,
saying, "Lord, help me!" But He answered and
said, "It is not good to take the children's bread
and throw it to the little dogs." And she said, "Yes,
Lord, yet even the little dogs eat the crumbs which
fall from their masters' table." Then Jesus answered
and said to her, "O woman, great is your faith! Let
it be to you as you desire." And her daughter was
healed from that very hour.

— MATTHEW 15:21-28 (NKJV)

In Matthew 15, as Jesus was traveling and ministering from town to town, a Gentile woman came to Him and cried out for mercy. This woman told Jesus that her daughter was "severely demon-possessed." Later in this passage, in verse 28, we are told that Jesus "healed" the woman's daughter. We might ask, "Are we dealing with some kind of demonic possession, or are we dealing with somebody who needs healing in their body?"

Which is it?

Some people often over-spiritualize situations. They believe a demon causes every problem and every need for healing requires the equivalent of an exorcism. Most of us know better than that. We understand that if someone is blind or deaf, it does not necessarily mean they have demons. If somebody has seizures or is paralyzed, it is not conclusive evidence they are possessed by an evil spirit. While it is true that some over-spiritualize every issue they encounter, there is also danger at the other end of the spectrum, too.

Again, it's certainly possible to hyper-spiritualize sickness and disease, but much of the church today has made a mistake in the other direction. There is a strong tendency to *under*-spiritualize things related to our health.

For many Christians, sickness and disease is just a matter of science; germs that you need medication to deal with or malignant cells that you need an operation to remove. It is science, nothing more and nothing less.

I do not mean this to be taken as an anti-doctor statement. Thank God for talented doctors. Thank God for the advances in the medical field. Good doctors are anti-sickness, and I am thankful for them. But as wonderful as doctors and medical science can be, it is important for us to understand and acknowledge that illness has a spiritual component. The Devil is ultimately behind all sickness and disease. Understanding that sickness has a spiritual root will help us see a spiritual solution's validity.

> And you know that God anointed Jesus of Nazareth
> with the Holy Spirit and with power. Then Jesus
> went around doing good and healing all who were
> oppressed by the devil, for God was with him.
>
> — ACTS 10:38 (NLT)

Jesus healed people with a wide variety of illnesses. He healed everything from fever to someone four days dead. He healed people with diseases affecting their blood and people with diseases affecting their skin. Jesus healed people who had seizures, who were blind, deaf, crippled, and more!

According to Acts 10:38, each person Jesus healed needed healing because they were oppressed by the Devil. It does not matter if it is cancer, the flu, the sniffles, or something hereditary; all sickness is oppression by the enemy. God did not design any form of sickness, and He never meant for you to suffer any of those things.

Let's look at another example:

> One Sabbath day as Jesus was teaching in a synagogue,
> he saw a woman who had been crippled by an evil
> spirit. She had been bent double for eighteen years
> and was unable to stand up straight. When Jesus
> saw her, he called her over and said, "Dear woman,
> you are healed of your sickness!" Then he touched
> her, and instantly she could stand straight. How
> she praised God!
>
> — LUKE 13:10-13 (NLT)

After Jesus healed this woman with a back problem, the religious leaders were upset. Because this healing took place on the Sabbath day, they complained and said the miracle should have been performed on a different day of the week. Within Jesus' response, we learn the ultimate cause of this woman's back problem.

Jesus did not attribute her back issue to poor posture or a failure to lift with her knees. Jesus did not say she was the victim of a bad mattress or bad genetics. Read Jesus' response:

> But the Lord replied, "You hypocrites! Each of you works on the Sabbath day! Don't you untie your ox or your donkey from its stall on the Sabbath and lead it out for water? This dear woman, a daughter of Abraham, has been held in bondage by Satan for eighteen years. Isn't it right that she be released, even on the Sabbath?"
>
> — LUKE 13:15, 16 (NLT)

Jesus said that the woman who had been doubled over for 18 years was being held in bondage by Satan. Her trouble was not simply the result of a slipped disk or osteoporosis, it had a spiritual root. Jesus understood there is a spiritual component to sickness, disease, and suffering. If it is a spiritual issue, then no amount of chiropractic adjustments, braces, or corrective shoes will adequately deal with the problem.

It is important for us to understand we are spiritual beings whom God has filled with his own Spirit and we are up against spiritual forces when we deal with sickness and disease. It is not just science and things better left to medical professionals. There is a significant spiritual component.

Acknowledging a spiritual component to sickness and disease does not mean every sick person is demon-possessed. Spiritual problems require spiritual solutions, and there is a spiritual aspect we need to be aware of. The Bible tells us the Spirit of God inside of us is greater than the one operating in the world (1 John 4:4). When you deal with sickness and understand its spiritual root, you become aware that you have something inside of you that is greater and more powerful than what you are up against.

God Is Pleased by Your Request

> Then Jesus went out from there and departed to the region of Tyre and Sidon. 22 And behold, a woman of Canaan came from that region and cried out to Him, saying, "Have mercy on me, O Lord, Son of David! My daughter is severely demon-possessed." But He answered her not a word. And His disciples came and urged Him, saying, "Send her away, for she cries out after us." But He answered and said, "I was not sent except to the lost sheep of the house of Israel." Then she came and worshiped Him, saying, "Lord, help me!"
>
> — MATTHEW 15:21-28 (NKJV)

The Gentile woman in Matthew 15 came to Jesus and cried out, "Have mercy on me, my daughter needs deliverance! My daughter needs healing!" After hearing her desperate plea, Jesus did not say a thing. He acted like she was not even there. Apparently, she continued crying out because the disciples got involved and said, "Jesus will you do something? She's driving us crazy. Get her out of here!"

Since this woman was a Gentile, Jesus said, "I was only sent to the house of Israel." In other words, because she was not an Israelite, she was on her own.

She persisted.

In verse 25, we are told that she continued to pursue healing and went before Jesus "worshiping Him." This is important; how did she worship Him? Did she begin singing a worship chorus? Does it say she started to play the organ or tambourine? Did she come before Him waving banners or flags? It does not say that any of those things happened. She worshiped Him by saying something. *What did she say?*

> Then she came and worshiped Him, saying, "Lord,
>   help me!"
>
> — MATTHEW 15:25 (NKJV)

This was her worship; "Lord, help me!" The Bible counts her plea for help as worship before Jesus. She came before him saying, "Jesus help me." Many people think God gets annoyed with our requests.

Maybe you have heard people say, "I know people have much worse problems than I do, I don't want to bother Him." Or maybe you have felt that way yourself.

Your need is not an annoyance to Jesus. It is not something that aggravates or bothers Him. In Matthew 15, we see someone persistently calling out for help, and it is counted as worship.

She came before Him saying, "Jesus you have what I need. Jesus, I have put my hope and my trust in You. You can do what no one else can do. You can handle this problem, so I'm coming to You." That was like a sweet fragrance rising up before the Lord, and He counted it as worship.

It is the same with you and me. When we go to the Lord seeking His help, whether it is a toothache or HIV, it is not an aggravation to Him. You are not inconveniencing God when you ask Him to get involved. It is received as worship when you say, "Jesus, You are able, I look to You, I trust You, You alone have what I need, and so I come before You seeking Your help." It is pleasing to Jesus. It is worship.

Understanding the Level of Bread

She came to Him, worshiping, saying, "Lord, help me."

Here is His response:

> But He answered and said, "It is not good to take the children's bread and throw it to the little dogs.
>
> — MATTHEW 15:26 (NKJV)

What in the world is Jesus talking about?

This woman is seeking healing. She wants deliverance for her daughter, whose life is on the line, and Jesus starts talking about *bread.*

Jesus is not off on an unrelated tangent or changing the subject. He is talking about the same thing she is talking about, but He is using an analogy. He is asked about healing and responds as follows:

"It is not good to take the children's bread..."

When Jesus said "the children's bread," He was talking about the healing this woman desired for her daughter.

Healing = the Children's Bread

Understanding Jesus' choice of analogy is important.

When a parent gives their child bread, it is considered a base level provision. If you are a parent, you probably do not consider providing a piece of bread for your child as a rare treat or indulgence. It is—simply put—basic.

You might not buy your children the latest technological gadget or expensive clothes; bread is nothing like those things. Bread is a basic, low-level provision. Jesus could have used any analogy. He could have used a food that is rarer and more special. He could have said, "It is not good to take the children's Thanksgiving turkey and give it to the dogs." He could have said, "It's not good to take the children's Christmas ham," or "It isn't right to take the children's lobster tails and caviar." He could have used some analogy that was not food and said, "It's not good to take the children's family heirloom; that valuable antique that has been passed down for generations, and throw it to the dogs."

Elsewhere, Jesus used analogies of things with great value. In Matthew 13, for example, Jesus talked about treasure hidden in a field worth selling everything to acquire. In the same chapter, He used the analogy of the "pearl of great price."

Jesus was adept when it came to analogies. He understood how to illustrate things that are rare and hard to find. He also understood how to illustrate things readily available to any child belonging to a decent parent. Jesus was well aware of the illustrations and analogies He used and their implications.

Relating healing to basic provision is not meant to diminish its value. We need to understand how God views healing for His children. It is not some rare, special treat for a couple of His favorites; it is base level provision. If you are a child of God, it is *your* bread; it belongs to <u>you</u>. Healing is not something we have to convince God to do. It is something He tells us belongs to His children.

My children have begged me for all kinds of things, but having a slice of bread has never been one of them. If you are a parent, your child has never had to get straight *A*s on their report card or jump through certain behavioral hoops to earn bread. Parents never say, "Be on your very best behavior, and who knows, maybe this Christmas will be the year you finally get the piece of bread you've been asking for." You may try to persuade and reward them with other items, but not bread.

Bread is basic provision.

Imagine I invited you over to my house and told you I was going to fix an amazingly extravagant dinner for you and told you to come hungry. Then the day comes for our dinner together. When you arrive at my house, I seat you in the dining room, then disappear into the kitchen to finish getting things ready. When I finally come out of the kitchen, I am carrying a plate with nothing but one slice of white bread. I set it in front of you and say, "Enjoy!"

What would you think?

I am sure you are a very gracious, polite person and you would probably enjoy the piece of bread and thank me for it. But if you invited me over to your house, told me you would prepare a special meal, and then put a slice of bread on my plate, I would not be as kind. I would not say, "Wow! You really went above and beyond! This is SO special!" I would be looking in the kitchen, wondering what was coming next. I would think, "Surely this isn't *all* there is." Why would I feel that way? Because bread is so simple. Bread is not the culmination of the meal, but something basic that goes along with it. Bread is not some extraordinarily rare item; it's something easily acquired.

Bread is base level provision, which is how God sees it. Too often, God's children do not see it that way. They see healing as something unusual and special. Believers view walking in divine health as something that must be begged for; something we must twist God's arm for. But Jesus called it the *children's bread.*

In Matthew 15:26, Jesus said, "It is not good to take the children's bread." In some translations it says, "it is not proper" or "it is not right." Healing is the children's bread, and it is not proper/not good/not right for them not to possess it.

According to Jesus' standard, anything in your life depriving you of health is improper. Anything, or anyone, trying to deny you the bread that God said is yours as His child is out of line with what Jesus Himself considers proper and in order. Whether a person, a teaching, a philosophy, or a doctrine; it is not acceptable to Jesus if it keeps God's children from having their bread.

If you know Jesus as your savior, then you are a child of God. Because you are a child of God, healing belongs to you. Healing is not just a special treat for a couple of God's kids. It is something that Jesus said is wrong for God's children to go without.

Bread is basic.

In no way is the idea of healing being "basic" meant to take away from how wonderful healing is. It is meant to align our point of view with God's. We miss out on healing when we think of it as some lofty thing God is very hesitant to distribute. It becomes difficult, if not impossible, to have faith for healing when it is viewed differently than how God views it. It is like bread for His children, and it is not good for them to not have it. That is how you must think of it.

Healing is yours. It belongs to you.

It is a base level provision in the Kingdom of God.

Healing Comes by Faith

> But He answered and said, "It is not good to take the
> children's bread and throw it to the little dogs."
> And she said, "Yes, Lord, yet even the little dogs eat
> the crumbs which fall from their masters' table."
> Then Jesus answered and said to her, "O woman,
> great is your faith! Let it be to you as you desire."
> And her daughter was healed from that very hour.
>
> — MATTHEW 15:26-28 (NKJV)

When Jesus told the woman that she could have the healing she desired, He attributed the healing to her faith. We cannot adequately deal with the subject of healing and not talk about the importance of faith.

Faith is absolutely necessary. Faith is critical to both walking in divine health and ministering healing to others. You see it in the story from Matthew 15 and throughout the ministry of Jesus. Reading through the Gospels, you find Jesus repeatedly telling people they have received their healing because of their faith.

The woman with the issue of blood in Mark 5 is a great example. After constant bleeding for 12 years, a woman heard about Jesus. She said to herself, "I know if I can just touch the edge of His garment, I'll be made whole." She fought her way through a crowd, touched Him, and received her healing. Jesus stopped and asked, "Who touched me?" The disciples said, "You've got to be kidding me; there are people everywhere." But Jesus knew someone had touched Him deliberately; He felt healing power go out of Him. The healed woman came, fell before Jesus, and confessed, "Lord, I touched you, and I received my healing." When Jesus heard what had happened, He credited her faith with the healing. He said, "Daughter, your faith has made you well." (Mark 5:34).

Faith plays a crucial role in receiving healing, walking in divine health, and ministering healing to others. People will try to explain away faith's importance, but as you read through the Word of God, you cannot escape the fact that faith plays an essential role in healing. It is so vital that Jesus noted faith as the sole reason for the woman's healing in Mark 5. Faith is so important that when it was absent in Jesus' hometown of Nazareth, we are told an absence of mighty miracles was the direct result (Mark 6:5).

Acknowledging the importance of faith brings personal responsibility. People will use experiences to downplay faith's importance. They might say, "My uncle Fred was sick, and he really believed. He never received his healing. I *know* he believed."

When there is a clash between someone's experience and the Word of God, learn to side with the Word of God.

Often, people will attempt to explain to themselves and others why healing did not take place. They may reason that God is trying to teach them something through the illness or that it is His will for some other motive. I have heard some say that God was just "not ready" to heal. These types of "explanations" put the responsibility on God by concluding He has some higher reason we don't understand for inflicting pain and disease on someone. We can try to lessen our responsibility by explaining things away, or we can take the attitude that says, "Whatever changes I need to make, I will make. My experience must line up with the Word of God. Jesus, if You say it takes faith, then I will build my faith instead of trying to explain it away!"

Determine not to bring God's Word down to the level of your experience, instead choose to bring your experience up to the standard of God's Word.

Placing emphasis on the importance of faith in healing makes people uncomfortable. Still, it is the reality found in the Word. If you strip away the parts of God's Word that make people uncomfortable, you will be left with very little. When people had faith, they were healed. When they did not have faith, they were not.

Understanding healing comes by faith also helps us to see healing is still for today. Many argue that healing and miracles were only for Jesus' time or for the early church. Those same people will acknowledge faith is still important in other areas like salvation. They will acknowledge that faith still comes from the Word of God. If people can still have faith and build faith, then people can also still be healed. If faith is still for today then healing is still for today as well.

The Provision has Been Made

The woman we have been discussing from Matthew 15 was in a more difficult spot than you and I, regarding faith for healing. She came to Jesus believing there was something He could do, and she was trying to get Him to do it. She had faith, saying, "Jesus, please do this, I know you are able." She believed that Jesus *could* heal her daughter. Now, you and I can build our faith on what the Bible tells us Jesus has *already* accomplished for us. Instead of believing Jesus *could* do something, the Bible tells us healing has *already* been purchased.

> Surely He has borne our griefs (sicknesses, weaknesses,
>   and distresses) and carried our sorrows and pains
>   [of punishment], yet we [ignorantly] considered
>   Him stricken, smitten, and afflicted by God [as if
>   with leprosy]. But He was wounded for our trans-
>   gressions, He was bruised for our guilt and iniqui-
>   ties; the chastisement [needful to obtain] peace and
>   well-being for us was upon Him, and with the

stripes [that wounded] Him we are healed and made whole.

— ISAIAH 53:4, 5 (AMP)

The last part of verse 5 in the New King James Version reads, "And by His stripes we are healed." The word translated "healed" in the Hebrew means to be full of health or to be repaired. It means to be fully healthy, or if something has gone wrong, if something is broken down and not working, to get it working again or repaired.

This passage from Isaiah 53 talks about what Jesus did on His way to the cross. By the beating He took, by every wound on his back, healing was provided. Jesus has already taken those stripes on His back, so provision has already been made. "Surely he has borne our sicknesses and carried our pains." For you and me, this is a past tense event. Jesus has already done it. When we need healing, it is not something we are trying to coax God into doing.

Everything necessary for our healing has already been provided by the sacrifice of Jesus. We are not trying to talk Jesus into taking one more sickness on himself. He already did it. That bread is already available. Healing is the children's bread. Now it is just a matter of us consuming it, and the way we do that is by faith.

CHAPTER 3
UNLIMITED SUPPLY

He who walks with wise men will be wise, but the
companion of fools will be destroyed.

— PROVERBS 13:20 (NKJV)

A s you read through the Word of God, especially the gospel accounts, pay attention to how stories are arranged. Often, the sequence of stories is used to emphasize certain points. You can read a portion of scripture and gain understanding from it. But sometimes, the stories are arranged so if considered in connection with one another, you see a larger point, or an emphasis added.

For example, in Mark chapter 8, there is a story of Jesus healing a blind man. Jesus laid hands on the man, then asked him if he could see anything. The man said he could see people but not very clearly; they looked like trees walking around. Jesus laid His hands on the man a second time, this time his vision was completely restored.

The very next story, beginning in verse 27, Jesus asks His disciples "Who do men say that I am?" People had a general idea that Jesus was a man of God. They thought He was John the Baptist, Elijah, or some other prophet. Jesus asked a second question, "Who do *you* say that I am?" Peter answered correctly, "You are the Christ."

Notice the parallels in these stories. In the first, the man could see, but not clearly. In the second, people had some ideas about Jesus being a godly man but were not clear about His true identity.

In the first story, Jesus laid hands on the man a second time, and the man's vision was completely restored, and he saw clearly. In the second story, Jesus asked a second question, and Peter was able to properly discern who Jesus is and identify Jesus clearly as the Christ.

The point is, not only do the individual stories in the Gospels matter, but the structure and sequence of the stories do as well.

In the passage we have been looking at from Matthew 15, Jesus introduced an analogy linking healing with bread; healing is the children's bread. With that connection in mind, let's read the next few verses.

> Jesus departed from there, skirted the Sea of Galilee, and went up on the mountain and sat down there. Then great multitudes came to Him, having with them the lame, blind, mute, maimed, and many others; and they laid them down at Jesus' feet, and He healed them. So the multitude marveled when they saw the mute speaking, the maimed made whole, the lame walking, and the blind seeing; and they glorified the God of Israel.
>
> — MATTHEW 15:29-31 (NKJV)

"Great multitudes" came to Jesus with a wide variety of health issues (lame, blind, mute, maimed, etc.). An emphasis is put on the incredible number of people. A multitude is a large number of people. Here it is used in the plural, "multitudes". But even that was not sufficient to highlight just how big the crowd really was, so *"great* multitudes" is used to emphasize what an overwhelming amount of people this was.

They came before Jesus, and Jesus began to heal the "great multitudes". People were rejoicing and glorifying God; mute people were talking, lame people were walking, and blind people were seeing. This continued day after day. For three straight days, Jesus placed His hands on the people and ministered healing to them.

> Now Jesus called His disciples to Himself and said, "I have compassion on the multitude, because they have now continued with Me three days and have nothing to eat. And I do not want to send them away hungry, lest they faint on the way." Then His disciples said to Him, "Where could we get enough bread in the wilderness to fill such a great multitude?"
>
> — MATTHEW 15:32, 33 (NKJV)

We will continue reading this passage but notice what the topic has now become—bread. Jesus linked bread and healing together when he dealt with the Gentile woman in verses 21-28. We then see an overwhelming flow of healing ministered to great multitudes of people in verses 29-31, and in verses 32-33, the focus has again become bread. This is not by accident.

> Jesus said to them, "How many loaves do you have?" And they said, "Seven, and a few little fish." So He commanded the multitude to sit down on the ground. And He took the seven loaves and the fish and gave thanks, broke them and gave them to His disciples; and the disciples gave to the multitude.

> So they all ate and were filled, and they took up
> seven large baskets full of the fragments that were
> left. Now those who ate were four thousand men,
> besides women and children. And He sent away
> the multitude, got into the boat, and came to the
> region of Magdala.
>
> — MATTHEW 15:34-39 (NKJV)

After 3 days of ministry, Jesus decides to feed the people, but the supplies are limited. He took 7 loaves of bread and a few fish and began to feed the people. We are told there were 4,000 men, not counting women and children. If every man had his wife with him and every family had just one child, that would be 12,000 people (12,000 is a conservative estimate. Families typically had more than one child. Also, 12,000 does not account for single women in the crowd). Jesus fed all 12,000+ people from the seven loaves. When it was all said and done, they had seven large baskets full of leftovers.

Why did they end up with so much food left over? Was Jesus not good at calculating how much food was going to be needed? Surely, He could have multiplied the exact amount of fish and loaves necessary to feed this crowd so there would not be a single crumb left over. But that is not what happened.

Interestingly, we are told how Jesus distributed the food. Jesus did not give thanks and then multiply the food all at once. It says He gave thanks, broke it, and then gave it to his disciples, and they took and administered it to the people. The disciples started waiting tables and delivering the food. Food for 12,000 people would have been too much to carry in one trip, so this was a process.

Jesus broke the bread, gave it to His disciples, and they carried it to the people. The disciples delivered the food then came back for more. That was the process. Jesus broke the bread; the disciples delivered it to the people and then returned to Jesus for more. This took a while given how many people there were to feed.

When the disciples had finally served all the people and let Jesus know everyone had been fed, Jesus did not stop making bread.

"Jesus, we said that's enough! Everyone has been fed!"

But Jesus kept making more until there were seven baskets extra. The number seven is significant in the story; seven baskets full. Seven is not a random number. Jesus wanted there to be seven.

In the Book of Daniel, when Nebuchadnezzar said, "Heat that furnace up seven times hotter," He was not instructing them to heat it to a specific temperature. He was not saying to get out a thermometer and take the fire from 1,000 to 7,000 degrees. When Nebuchadnezzar said "Make it seven times hotter" he was telling his servants to make the furnace as hot as possible; he knew his servants understood that. Seven indicates completion or perfection. Saying "Make it seven times hotter" meant "Get the furnace as hot as possible; completely hot, perfectly hot."

In Matthew 18, Peter asked Jesus, "Lord, how often should I forgive someone who sins against me? Seven times?" Peter was not being petty by proposing the number 7. He was asking about forgiving completely. Jesus' response, that we should forgive 70x7, shows just how thorough and perfect His forgiveness really is.

In Matthew 15, Jesus wanted seven baskets of left-over bread because when it comes to healing, there is an unlimited supply. Healing is the children's bread. No matter what your condition, or how long you've had it, it is impossible to exhaust the resources that God has. You cannot stretch Him; you cannot push the envelope and get God to a point where He is uncomfortable. There is an unlimited supply, a complete supply, a perfect supply of bread for His children. He goes above and beyond. Seven baskets left over. Seven is the number of perfection and completion which describes the health God desires for you and your family. Perfectly, completely, abundantly healthy.

2 Keys the Gentile Woman Grasped

> But He answered and said, "I was not sent except to the
> lost sheep of the house of Israel." Then she came
> and worshiped Him, saying, "Lord, help me!" But
> He answered and said, "It is not good to take the
> children's bread and throw it to the little dogs."
> And she said, "Yes, Lord, yet even the little dogs eat
> the crumbs which fall from their masters' table."
>
> — MATTHEW 15:24-27 (NKJV)

This Gentile woman's high level of confidence in the power of *"the bread,"* was key to receiving her healing. When Jesus said, "It is not good to take the children's bread and throw it to the little dogs," she was not moved. Instead of becoming discouraged, the Gentile woman simply requested that a crumb of bread might be allowed to fall to her. She was certain about the effectiveness of the bread and knew even a crumb was more than enough to do the job. She did not need a loaf or two. Just a touch was enough to set her daughter free and reverse whatever condition the enemy had afflicted her with.

Similarly, the woman with the issue of blood said, "If I may but touch the *hem* of His garment." She understood that sickness is no match for the power of God!

In Matthew 8, a Roman centurion said to Jesus, "I am not worthy that You should come under my roof. But only speak a word, and my servant will be healed."

One word. One touch. One crumb.

Do not be more confident in sickness than in God's power to heal. People often magnify how deadly a disease is or how bad a diagnosis is. The three examples referenced above did the complete opposite. They made little of the power of sickness and much of God's power. Their confidence was not misplaced. Each of them received their miracle.

The second key the Gentile woman from Matthew 15 grasped was having confidence in what belonged to her. After she pleaded with Jesus for healing, He said, "Listen, it's not right to take the bread from children and give it to the little dogs." Even at dog status, the woman knew what belonged to her.

"True, you've made a good point:" she said, "I can't really argue with you there. But you know what *does* belong to the dogs? The crumbs that fall off the table are fair game. If I'm a dog, then the crumbs are mine!" If she was aware of what belonged to her as a dog, how much more confident should those of us who are God's children be in what belongs to us?

The Bible says God prepares a table before you in the spiritual realm. On that table is a loaf of bread that brings healing to your body. It belongs to you, and it is not only for a few. There is plenty to go around. It is base level provision in the family of God.

A healthy, strong body, with all your organs functioning properly, your ears hearing clearly, your eyes seeing clearly, every joint functioning properly, it belongs to you! God wants to see you live out all your days with a healthy, strong body.

> Now Jesus called His disciples to Himself and said, "I
> have compassion on the multitude because they
> have now continued with Me three days and have

nothing to eat. And I do not want to send them
away hungry, lest they faint on the way.

— MATTHEW 15:32 (NKJV)

Jesus provided bread for the multitude out of compassion. He knew the people were hungry and did not want to send them away in that condition "lest they faint on the way." He was aware there was a need and was going to make the necessary provision.

Why not just send them away hungry? Why not tell them to eat when they get home? Jesus did not want them to faint on their way.

Wherever it was they were going, wherever the road was going to take them, Jesus wanted them to go healthy, strong, and well-nourished. "I don't want them to faint. I don't want them growing weary. I don't want them to fall down or stumble because their body isn't strong enough." Jesus' desire to provide bread to those people is the same desire He has to provide healing to you. He does not want you to limp through life. It is not His desire to see you faint, growing weary, unable to walk the course He has marked for you. Healing belongs to you. It is the children's bread.

Just a few chapters earlier, Jesus asked His listeners some questions about a father giving his child bread:

"Or what man is there among you who, if his son asks
for bread, will give him a stone? Or if he asks for a
fish, will he give him a serpent?"

— MATTHEW 7:9, 10 (NKJV)

When Jesus made this statement, He was not unaware of the connection between healing and bread. If you are a parent and your child asks you for some bread, would you give them some kind of terrible substitute and just say, "That's your lot in life, you've got to deal with it"?

If your child asked, "Can I have a fish?" would you give them something harmful instead of something nourishing? Of course not!

People often believe that way about their heavenly Father. Some are convinced God wants to deny them healing or inflict them with some kind of suffering, and somehow, it is pleasing to Him. Jesus said when a child asks a good father for bread the father responds by giving it to them. Healing is the children's bread.

CHAPTER 4

MAKE SURE YOU HAVE WHAT IS YOURS

If you are a child of God, healing is already yours. It is an established spiritual reality. It has already been purchased for you and is yours based on the provision of Jesus. But just like everything else in the Kingdom, we must appropriate it, or claim it, by faith. This is true for everything in the New Covenant. For example, in Ephesians 5:8, Paul wrote, "For you were once darkness, but now you are light in the Lord. Walk as children of light."

Paul was writing to the church in Ephesus, giving instructions to get them straightened out in their behavior. He was trying to get them to live righteously. They should have already been walking in holiness, but they were not. In Ephesians chapter 5, Paul wrote about a variety of behavioral issues. He addressed people who were stealing from others and dealt with the way they talked to one another. He went on to deal with relationships between husbands and wives, kids and parents, and employees and employers. Paul was trying to get their lives lined up with God's will for them.

In Ephesians 5:8, he told them, "...you were once darkness..." That was the way they *used* to be. That *had been* their reality. But because they accepted Jesus, he told them, "...you are now light... walk as children of light."

It is important to notice Paul did *not* say, "Listen guys, if you want to be light, you better get your act together. You need to get on the ball! This behavior isn't going to cut it. You're never going to reach light status living the way you're living." No, he did not say any of those things. He told them their spiritual reality; *you are* light. Then he told them to live like it. He was instructing them to begin living in line with a spiritual truth established by the work of Jesus.

Having a clear understanding of who you are and what is yours in the Kingdom is key to producing the right behavior.

> For you were once darkness, but now you are light in
> the Lord. Walk as Children of light.
>
> — EPHESIANS 5:8 (NKJV)

Ephesians 5 reveals that someone can accept Jesus and become light but continue to live as if they were darkness. On the other hand, if they choose to, they can build their faith and claim the spiritual reality of being light; "Lord, I know in Jesus I have been made a child of light. God, I know the power of sin is broken in my life. I am no longer a slave to sin. Father, I thank you that in Jesus, you set me free, and I am the righteousness of God in Christ."

If the Ephesians had grabbed the truth and reality of the spiritual realm by faith and established it in their hearts, they could have walked it out in their daily lives. They could seize the provision of freedom and right-eousness and actually experience it. It had already been established in the spiritual realm. They *were* light. They *were* righteousness. But just because it is a spiritual reality does not mean it was observed or enjoyed in their lives. They needed to intentionally claim it by faith. This applies to you and me as well.

In the Kingdom of God, you are given a certain status or reality (light, righteousness, healed, etc.) and are to live a life consistent with that status. The problem for many people is that things work the opposite way in the natural world. In the natural, you must live a certain way to reach a certain status or reality. In the natural, a person's status is based on how they live, but in the Kingdom of God, we are to live and behave based on our fixed spiritual status.

For example: If I said I wanted to have the status of being a world-class pro athlete, what would need to happen? I would need some degree of natural talent and to train very hard. Ideally, I would begin developing my skills while I was young. More than likely, I would need to excel in high school, then do well on a college team. From there, I would make it into the pros. To be considered world-class, I would need to continue to excel at the pro level. Eventually, maybe I could finally become known as world-class. My status/reality would be entirely based on my behavior and how I perform.

Or suppose I wanted to reach the status of being a great businessman; what would I have to do? I would need to learn a lot about business, get a job and climb the corporate ladder. Maybe start my own business, and eventually, after a lot of success and earning a lot of money, I could achieve the reality of being a wealthy, successful businessman. That status/reality would be based entirely on my behavior and performance. In God's Kingdom, however, my behavior is supposed to be based on the status/reality that He has already given me.

Isaiah 53 tells us Jesus already bore our sicknesses and disease. It says He has already carried our pain, and by His stripes we have been declared healed. This is an important truth that applies in many areas, and healing is certainly one of them. Your healing is already established as a spiritual fact. Now you must determine to grab onto that provision by faith and make it your own experience. This is what it means to walk by faith.

Romans 4 talks about Abraham, the father of faith. It tells us how steadfast he was in believing God for a son. He believed God would make his body fruitful, even though it was as good as dead concerning reproduction. Abraham counted God faithful. As years passed, his faith did not diminish; it actually grew stronger. Abraham was not considering natural circumstances, he was walking by faith.

Verse 17 of that chapter gives insight into how God operates. Romans 4:17 says that God is the one "who quickeneth the dead, and calleth those things which be not as though they were." That is how God operates. He does not operate by what is seen. "He calls those things which be not as though they were." He does not disregard things when they are no longer alive; He causes life to return. He makes what is dead come back to life. With Abraham and Sarah, He took dead reproductive organs that had never produced and caused them to come alive and bring forth a son.

God changed Abraham's name from Abram to Abraham. The Hebrew word Abraham means father of a multitude. God began to call this childless man "father of a multitude" before he had any children. Why did God call him "father of a multitude"? Because He calls those things which be not as though they *were*. He was calling it into existence. When God declares something, it becomes a reality. Just like when He created light; He spoke it, and it came into existence.

When God called Abram "father of a multitude" it was established in the spiritual realm. In God's heart, it was settled, "this guy is the father of multitudes; he's the father of many nations." It was set in God's mind.

The only way Abraham could experience what God said was to believe that God knew what He was talking about. He considered God faithful. That is walking by faith. This is the way God works, and it pleases Him when we have faith. Hebrews 11:6 tells us, "Without faith it is impossible to please God."

God "calleth those things which be not as though they were." Some will discourage you from calling yourself healed when you are experiencing symptoms. They think it is lying to call yourself whole even though you may have a headache. It is not lying; it is calling those things that are not as though they were.

In The Book of Revelation, Jesus is referred to as the lamb who was slain *from the foundation of the world* (Revelation 13:8). But wait a minute, slain from the foundation of the world? When was Jesus actually crucified? According to the Bible, Jesus was slain long after the creation story in Genesis 1 and 2. How does God get away with saying that Jesus was slain from the foundation, or from the very beginning, of the world?

Because in the spiritual realm, it was already a done deal. It was already established, but it took some time for it to manifest in the physical realm. In the heart of God, Jesus was the lamb that was slain long before those Roman soldiers nailed Him to the cross. That's the way we must operate, by faith. Faith understands there are spiritual realities that have not yet manifested in the natural. It takes faith to appropriate these spiritual realities and bring them into the physical realm.

God was pleased with the faith of the woman in Matthew 15. When Jesus saw how strong her faith was, He said with a smile, "Woman, great is your faith, I love the way you believe, let it be to you as you have desired."

What Does it Mean to Walk By Faith?

For we walk by faith, not by sight.

— 2 CORINTHIANS 5:7

(NKJV)

God desires that you walk by faith and NOT by sight. If you walk by one, you *cannot* walk by the other. They are mutually exclusive. That means the moment you start walking by sight, you stop walking by faith. It is either one or the other. Walking by what you feel, what you see, and what you can sense in the natural is walking by sight.

What does it mean to walk by faith? To receive the Word of God, just like Abraham, and believe it is true; live like it is true. Regarding healing, no matter how I feel, no matter what the doctors are telling me, no matter what symptoms exist, I believe God! By Jesus' stripes, I am healed!

This is the attitude we must take: "Whatever affliction is coming on my body; my pancreas not working, tumors growing in my body, aches, pains, etc.... Jesus, I know that you already carried this; you already bore this for me, so I don't have to. I know that healing belongs to me. I walk by faith."

We must keep our faith engaged in our prayer life. In Mark 11:24 Jesus said, "Therefore I say to you, whatever things you ask when you pray, believe you receive them, and you will have them." When it comes to prayer, Jesus said to believe you have received—when? *When you pray.* Believe it is already yours. Believe you *have* received, and what will happen? You will have them (the things that you prayed for).

The mistake many people make is they hold off believing until they have what they've prayed for. Jesus said to believe it is yours "when you pray." You believe it is already settled; "I know in the spiritual realm it's already a done deal, and by faith, I am calling it into the material/natural realm." You walk by faith and not by sight.

Once you see something, faith is eliminated. If you wait until you see a physical manifestation, you are walking by sight, not faith, which means it is no longer pleasing to God.

For example, my family and I live in West Virginia. My wife will sometimes take our kids and visit her parents in North Carolina without me. When she takes them to North Carolina, I believe that is where she is going, even though I do not actually see her there. I never worry that she secretly took our children to a babysitter and flew to Las Vegas. I believe her when she says she is in North Carolina. I trust my wife. I have faith in her.

Suppose on one of her visits to North Carolina I decide to check up on her and make sure she is where she says she is. I decide to drive through the night to North Carolina and do a surprise visit to ensure she is at her parent's house. I arrive bleary-eyed from driving and barge through the door of her parents' home to find my wife and my children all there. Faith is no longer an option. I can't honestly tell my wife I had faith in her the whole time because I had to see it to believe it. I am no longer in faith; I am relying on sight. It was only faith when I could not see it, and I believed anyway.

That is what God desires of us, faith. Without faith, pleasing God is an impossibility. God wants us to believe before we see, before we get our hands on it, before we feel it in our body.

"God I know I've already received it. It's an established fact. Father, I praise You. I thank You for it. I am healed! Healing belongs to me. I know it is the children's bread. You've already made provision, and I thank You for it."

We walk by faith and not by sight. It is either one or the other. Hebrews 11:6 tells us that without faith it is impossible to please God. Without faith it is impossible to please God. That means all the right conduct, holy living, watching your mouth, watching your behavior, etc., on their own, are not pleasing to God. Those are all good things, but if you are not walking in faith, none of it is pleasing to God. It is impossible to please God if you are not in faith.

Paul told Timothy we must fight the good fight of faith (1 Timothy 6:12). That means there is a battle involved in walking in faith. There is a war going on concerning whether you walk by faith or walk by sight.

To walk by faith, you must fight. You must build yourself up with the Word of God and prepare to handle conflict. When sense knowledge tells you something contrary to what God's Word says, that is where the battle takes place. The things you feel, see, and hear, will all battle to convince you God's Word is wrong. This is when you must fight the good fight of faith. Only fighters can lay hold of all that God has for them.

> Resist the devil and he will flee from you.
>
> — JAMES 4:7B (NKJV)

The Greek word translated "resist" in James 4:7 means "to resist by actively opposing pressure or power." When symptoms come and begin to afflict your body, there is a battle taking place.

Will you resist the enemy or just go by your feelings and accept whatever he is trying to afflict you with?

Nobody walks in divine health by accident.

No one walks in the spirit accidentally.

You won't walk according to the Word unopposed.

It takes someone who has set their face like flint (Isaiah 50:7), someone determined to fight the fight of faith. The Devil only flees from people who resist.

Our mindset must be: "I will fight the good fight of faith! I'm going to claim that bread. It is mine in Jesus' name. Just like the woman in Matthew 15, I'm not going anywhere without bread from that table because I know it belongs to me. I'm going to fight the good fight of faith and lay hold of what belongs to me."

CHAPTER 5
THE WORD PRECEDES HEALING

Oh, the joys of those who do not follow the advice of
the wicked, or stand around with sinners, or join in
with mockers. But they delight in the law of the
LORD, meditating on it day and night. They are
like trees planted along the riverbank, bearing fruit
each season. Their leaves never wither, and they
prosper in all they do.

— PSALMS 1:1-3 (NLT)

Healing is not something God must be talked into. Many feel the need to persuade God into healing, when it has already been made available. In fact, God desires to persuade *you* to be healed. He wants to convince *you* of His will through His Word and persuade you that healing is like bread for His children. If you are a child of God, healing belongs to you.

Many consider healing the spiritual equivalent of finding a 4-leaf clover. It is viewed as such a rare commodity that you must be in the right place, at the right time, and be one of the lucky few or one of the "chosen ones" to obtain healing.

That is not God's view at all. God considers it the children's bread. Bread is base level provision. No parent you know makes their child earn straight A's, beg, plead, wring their hands, do all their chores, and be on their best behavior to obtain a slice of bread. When a parent gives their child bread, it is not a special treat; it is basic provision. We must renew our minds to God's way of thinking regarding healing.

We receive things from the Word of God by faith. In Matthew 9:29, Jesus said, "It shall be done to you according to your faith." When people believe that healing is very unusual, hard to come by, and rarely occurs, that is exactly what it becomes in their life. When someone with that kind of mindset needs healing, they find themselves wishing, hoping and crossing their fingers instead of believing.

Healing is part of the atonement. Any sickness or disease that tries to attack your body is a sickness or disease that Jesus already carried in His body. Isaiah 53 tells us, that along with carrying your sins, mistakes, and shortcomings, Jesus also carried your sicknesses. It says, "Surely, He has borne our pains and carried our diseases." Jesus has already taken them on Himself so that you don't have to carry them. The price for your healing was paid in full almost 2000 years ago.

Child of God, healing belongs to you. It is not right for you to limp through this life, but you've got to be willing to fight for it. You must fight the good fight of faith (1 Timothy 6:12).

Obtaining anything by faith requires a fight. You have to get angry. Refuse to accept anything the enemy wants to put on you. Sickness is an enemy, not to be accommodated but to be fought. It is a thief. Sickness comes on people to make life difficult or unbearable. It comes to rob you of your potential. Sickness steals moments you could experience with your friends and memories you could make with your spouse. Infirmity desires to limit your enjoyment of life. Understand its intent and let it make you angry enough to fight back.

You must get stirred up to "lay hold of that for which Christ Jesus has also laid hold of you" (Philippians 3:12). Every time sickness comes on your body, time with your children is stolen. When you would love to be out in the backyard playing with them, but your stomach is bothering you, or you have another migraine. Whatever the symptoms are, sickness comes to rob you of fulfillment. It seeks to rob you of the very thing Jesus came to give you—LIFE! Learn to hate it and, in doing so, love the atonement. Love the finished work of Jesus! By His stripes you are healed.

The Word As Bread For Healing

> Then Jesus was led up by the Spirit into the wilderness to be tempted by the devil. And when He had fasted forty days and forty nights, afterward He was hungry. Now when the tempter came to Him, he said, "If You are the Son of God, command that these stones become bread." But He answered, "It is written, 'Man shall not live by bread alone, but by every word that proceeds from the mouth of God.'"
>
> — MATTHEW 4:1-4 (NKJV)

When Jesus was led into the wilderness and fasted for 40 days, the Devil came and began to tempt Him. With the first temptation, the Devil suggested Jesus turn a stone into bread to satisfy His hunger. Jesus responded by quoting Deuteronomy 8 and said, "Man does not live by bread alone, but by every word that comes from the mouth of God."

This means that people who only care for the physical aspects of their lives are not *really* living. How do we live if we cannot live by bread alone?

We live by the Word of God. People who are not feeding themselves with the Word of God, according to Jesus, are not really alive. There is another level of life beyond having a pulse. There is eternal, abundant, overflowing, everlasting life that is only obtained by the Word. Real life is only accessed through the Words that come from God.

When Jesus quoted Deuteronomy 8, He drew a parallel between physical bread and the Word of God. The idea of the Word of God being "bread" is consistent with other scripture passages. For example, in John 6:35, Jesus said, "I am the bread of life." Earlier in the Gospel of John, Jesus is identified as the Word of God (John 1:1-2,14). In John 6:35, the Word of God personally identified Himself as the Bread of Life.

> My son, give attention to my words; Incline your ear to
> my sayings. Do not let them depart from your eyes;
> Keep them in the midst of your heart; For they are
> life to those who find them, And health to all their
> flesh.
>
> — PROVERBS 4:20-22 (NKJV)

Proverbs 4:22 says that God's Words are "life to those who find them." But if you are reading the Word of God and studying the scriptures, then obviously, you are already alive. It is very difficult for a dead person to read the scriptures. So, this verse is not talking about simply having a heartbeat and being physically alive. It talks about spiritual life, as we read in Matthew chapter four. This life is only accessed by the Word of God.

Verse 22 goes on to say that while the Word of God provides us with spiritual life, it also can minister to us in the physical realm. Verse 22 says God's Words are, "life to those who find them, and health to all their flesh."

The Word of God is certainly beneficial to a person spiritually. But it does not stop there. Health is also provided. Just in case the reader may be overly spiritual, this verse states clearly where God's Word brings health; "health to all their flesh." Health for your body is obtained through the Word of God.

God's Word as Medicine

> For they are life unto those that find them and medicine to all their flesh.
>
> — PROVERBS 4:22 (JUBILEE BIBLE)

The Bible tells us that the Word of God has medicinal value. God's Word can provide health and healing, and, like any other medicine, there is a proper way to use it.

If your doctor gives you a prescription so you can get well, you must actually use it to receive the benefits of the medicine. But when you use the medicine, you cannot just do whatever you want with it. If your doctor prescribed a special skin cream, you cannot decide to consume three tablespoons of it and expect to get the desired results. No, you must follow the directions that come with the prescription, and the same is true with the Word of God.

God's Word is medicine, and thankfully, it comes without any ridiculous side effects that are worse than the condition you are trying to treat.

What is the prescription/directions?

My child, pay attention to what I say. Listen carefully
to my words.

— PROVERBS 4:20 (NLT)

The first part of the prescription is "pay attention". Sometimes we think the benefits of serving God are freely received, and in a sense, they are. But this verse reveals a price that must be paid for the life and health available in the Word of God. The cost you must pay is your attention.

For many, the price is too steep. If you are unwilling to pay attention to the Word of God you disqualify yourself from obtaining the life and the health located there.

"The secret of focus is elimination."

— DR. HOWARD
HENDRICKS

To pay attention, you must remove distractions. You need to eliminate the other things competing for your attention. Talking to someone while they are on their phone or watching TV can be very frustrating, especially if the message you want to communicate is important. For the message to be received clearly, the distraction must be eliminated. The phone must be set aside. The book must be laid down. The TV needs to be turned off. As long as their attention is divided, you do not have it.

If you remember a time, maybe in high school or college, when you had an important test that you needed to study for, where did you go to study? When it was time to get ready for that final exam, you did not take your books and study at the mall food court or an arcade. You knew you needed to pay attention, so you found a quiet place. You went to the library or some other location where you knew distractions would be minimal. Why? Because the secret of focus, or the secret of paying attention, is eliminating distractions. The same thing is true for paying attention to the Word of God.

When you study the Word of God daily, it is good to eliminate distractions and get alone. But we are not discussing daily devotional time; our focus is on obtaining healing. When you want to pay attention to God's Word, you must eliminate other factors. That means other "voices" that say things contrary to God's Word, need to be eliminated.

God's Word says, "Healing belongs to you. By His stripes you are healed." Eliminate voices that run contrary to that truth. Friends or family members may say things like, "You know what? Your Dad had that same thing. I guess it's just something everyone in our family comes down with …"

Choose to pay attention to the Word of God. You cannot pay attention to two separate things heading in opposite directions. There will be different voices competing for your attention concerning your health. Friends, family, doctors, even your own body, may all have something to say. You must decide where you will *pay* your attention.

Realize you cannot divide your attention equally and still say, "I'm paying attention." When you give heed to "voices" that disagree with what the Bible says, you have stopped paying the price to access what God has provided for you. Budget your attention properly and pay it to the Word of God.

The average Christian in the United States reads their Bible about once a month. That is not paying attention. If you were told I interacted with my children about once a month, your response would *not* be,

"What an attentive, devoted father!" You would think, "What a lazy, deadbeat, neglectful dad," and you would be right! Interacting with my child once a month, or even once a week, is not paying attention; it is neglecting. It is true when applied to parenting, and also true with our relationship to the Word of God.

One reason there is so much sickness in the Body of Christ is the lack of attention paid to the Word. Again, paying attention to the Word requires eliminating other opposing influences. Jesus operated this way. Sometimes Jesus clearly eliminated outside voices that came against the healing power that He was walking in.

In Mark 5, Jesus was on His way to heal Jairus' daughter. Before arriving at the little girl's home, the report came: "It's too late. She's already dead. Don't bother wasting Jesus' time." Jesus overheard what Jairus was told. In verse 36, Jesus said, "Don't be afraid. Just have faith." Jesus was instructing not to pay attention to what others were saying. Jairus needed to eliminate those voices and focus on what Jesus said He would do.

When they arrived at Jairus' house, they found people weeping and mourning. Before Jesus ministered to the little girl, he kicked everyone out except the girl's parents and three of His disciples. The mourners were present to comfort the family, considering what had happened, but Jesus had them removed. Why? Jesus was eliminating every voice of doubt. Every mocker that opposed the Word had to go. We must do the same thing in our lives. Jesus did not even allow for those expressing sympathy over what had happened. Sometimes even those who sympathize with a diagnosis or condition need to be eliminated. Do not accept comfort in a place you are not planning to stay.

The Word says you are healed. The Word says healing is yours. Do not let anyone distract your attention from what God's Word says about you, even well-meaning friends and family.

The prescription given in Proverbs 4:20 calls for you to pay attention to the Word.

> "The word says that you are healed. Get used to acting
> on the word."
>
> — E.W. KENYON

Make it a habit to live according to the truth of God's Word. Refuse to allow people's experiences or even how you feel to be more influential in your life than the Word. The Word should trump everything else in your life. The Word of God says you are healed. Learn to live and act like it's true. Make truth the base of operation in your life.

> My son, give attention to my words; Incline your ear to
> my sayings. Do not let them depart from your eyes;
> Keep them in the midst of your heart;
>
> — PROVERBS 4:20, 21 (NKJV)

The word "incline" used in this verse involves positioning yourself. It means to stretch out. It also means to pitch, as in pitching a tent. When the Bible talks about someone pitching an actual tent, it uses the same word that is used here.

For example, in Genesis 12:8, Abram "pitched his tent with Bethel on the west and Ai on the east." That verse tells us where Abram set up camp; that is where Abram settled in.

That is exactly what we are told to do concerning the Word of God in Proverbs 4:20. When you hear what the Word of God says, that is where you need to "set up camp." Find God's truth concerning your healing and decide, "This is where I'm going to settle. I am setting up camp here. I'm going to live from this place." Incline your ear. Hear the

Word of God, and then camp out right there. In John 15, Jesus said, "If you abide in me, and my words abide in you..."

When you hear the Word of God, pay attention, then choose to abide there. Refuse to "move away" from the Word of God.

Do not allow God's Word to depart from your eyes. You need to keep focused. When you envision what your life will look like, do not let His Word depart from your eyes. Keep that vision in line with His Word.

Hebrews 12:2 tells us to fix our eyes on Jesus, the author, or the initiator and the perfecter of our faith. Keeping your eyes on Jesus means keeping your eyes on the Word of God.

What does the Bible say about *your* situation?

Keep your eyes right there.

> God, who at various times and in various ways spoke in
> time past to the fathers by the prophets, has in
> these last days spoken to us by His Son...
>
> — HEBREWS 1:1, 2 (NKJV)

God has spoken to us through Jesus. What kinds of things did He do in his ministry? Jesus said, "If you have seen me, you have seen the Father" (John 14:9). He was the expressed will of God; literally, the living Word of God. You never read of Jesus making someone sick.

There is not a single instance of someone coming and asking Jesus for healing and being turned away.

There is never one time where Jesus said, "You know what? I think you've got a thing or two to learn before you come out of this." Or, "You know what? I think God's just blessed you with this sickness to straighten you out and to enlighten you." Not one single time did that ever happen. We are told to keep our eyes on Jesus. We are told that God speaks through Jesus, and when we see Him, we see what God's will is.

> My son, give attention to my words; Incline your ear to my sayings. Do not let them depart from your eyes; Keep them in the midst of your heart;
>
> — PROVERBS 4:20, 21 (NKJV)

Keep them. Keep what? Keep the Words of God. Keep them in the midst of your heart. The word "keep" has a few different meanings. One of them is to hold onto, or retain. You are to retain the Word of God. When you give it your attention and fix your eyes on it, make sure to *keep* it.

In James chapter one, God's Word is compared to a mirror. James tells us about someone who studies the Word of God, but then fails to *keep* it. He says that person is like somebody who looks at themselves in a mirror, but then they forget what they saw.

Imagine that you are out for lunch with some friends. You excuse yourself to use the restroom and while in the restroom you look in the mirror. As you look at yourself in the mirror, you notice your hair is a mess. Not only does your hair need some attention, but you also see something stuck in your teeth and somehow, you've got food smeared all around your mouth. You are slightly embarrassed about your appearance and realize that you need to fix some things before rejoining your friends. You glance away from the mirror, and as soon as you do, you completely forget everything you just saw in the mirror and make no changes. You rejoin your friends with a rat nest for hair and food still around your mouth and in your teeth. That would be foolishness, but James tells us people make this exact mistake when it comes to God's Word.

When you study the Word of God, or take time to read anointed books, and see that the Bible clearly tells us that healing belongs to God's children, don't walk away, forgetting what you saw. You see, in God's Word, healing is yours. God desires you to be well. When you look in that mirror, you see yourself as healthy and strong. How foolish to close your Bible, walk away and not live in line with what you saw. You have to retain it. Keep it in the midst of your heart. So the word "keep" means to hold on to, to retain.

The word "keep" also means to live in line with or regard it as true. When people *keep* the ten commandments, that doesn't mean they have just latched onto them and remembered them. If they "keep" the commandments, they are living in response to and in line with them. They regard them as true and obey them. We are supposed to keep God's Word, live in line with it, and regard it as true. We believe what His Word says and live our lives accordingly.

> Do not let them depart from your eyes; Keep them in the midst of your heart;
>
> — PROVERBS 4:21 (NKJV)

Keep it where? Not in a notebook. Not in a journal. "Keep them in the midst of your heart." When it says keep it in your heart, it is not about the blood-pumping muscle in your chest. It is talking about your inner man, your spirit being. You keep God's Word there. Regard it as true in your spirit man, because that's where healing initiates. Before you see a physical manifestation of the healing, it begins on the spiritual level. Keep God's Word, not in any old place. You are first to keep it in your inner man, because the physical is a manifestation of the spiritual.

Things in the physical realm are manifestations of what occurs in the spiritual realm. You can trace this truth back to creation. In John 4:24 Jesus said, "God is Spirit, and those who worship Him must worship in spirit and truth." One of the things we can learn from this verse is that God is a spirit being.

We know from the creation account, and other passages like John 1:3 and Revelation 4:11, that God created everything we see. God, who is spirit, spoke everything in the physical realm into existence. So, everything physical is a manifestation of what has occurred in the spiritual realm.

This same truth applies to your healing. It begins on the spiritual level because that is where we believe. Some people want to wait until they feel something, until they see something, or until they sense something, to believe healing has taken place. That is the same kind of attitude Thomas had in John 20. Thomas said, "Until I can stick my fingers into Jesus' side, until I can touch Him, until I can see Him, I won't believe." When Jesus showed up, He was not impressed with Thomas. Jesus did not say, "Way to go, Thomas. You're a levelheaded, practical-thinking, guy. I appreciate that about you." No, Jesus rebuked Him and said, "You only believe because you've seen, but blessed are those who believe before they see." Believing before you have the physical proof is the essence of faith.

This is the way people receive salvation as well. Healing and salvation both come from the same atoning work of Jesus, so it should not surprise us that we obtain them the same way. Romans 10:9 says, "If you confess with your mouth the Lord Jesus and believe in your heart God has raised Him from the dead, you will be saved."

To experience salvation, you must first do 2 things; confess with your mouth and believe in your heart. You can't say, "I'm going to wait to see if I'm really saved. I'll wait until I die and see if I actually go to Heaven." No, you believe in your heart or on a spiritual level, then you are saved. The next verse of Romans 10 says, "For with the heart one believes unto righteousness." You believe in your heart. That is where the process begins. Then what happens? After believing in your heart, you become righteous.

We receive salvation and become righteous by first believing in our heart. We receive healing the same way.

Before the woman with the issue of blood touched Jesus' garment to receive healing in Matthew 9, she said within herself, or she said in her heart, "If I can just touch the edge of his garment, I know I'll be healed." It was already settled in her heart. She believed in her healing long before it manifested. Before Jesus stopped and said, "Who touched my clothes," before she felt her bleeding stop, before any of those things happened, something was already settled in her innermost being. She said within herself, "I know if I can just touch Him, all I need is a touch from Jesus, and my case will be completely changed forever." And that is exactly what happened. There was a physical manifestation directly related to what she was "keeping" in her heart.

> My son, give attention to my words; Incline your ear to my sayings. Do not let them depart from your eyes; Keep them in the midst of your heart; For they are life to those who find them, and health to all their flesh.
>
> — PROVERBS 4:20-22 (NKJV)

God's Word is life and health to somebody. His Word does not provide life and health to everyone, but to a select group. They are life to *those who find them*. To be able to keep something in the midst of your heart, first, you need to find it. You can't pay attention to something you've never seen. You can't camp out, or set up camp someplace you've never discovered. God's Word provides life and health to people who find them.

The word "find" means to locate, discover, or come to. To come to what? To locate what? To discover, locate or "come to" the Word of God. To follow the other parts of this "prescription" it is necessary to be someone who "comes" to the Word.

When receiving salvation, you first have to "find" the Word of God. You need somebody to tell you what the Bible says. "But how can they call on him to save them unless they believe in him? And how can they believe in him if they have never heard about him? And how can they hear about him unless someone tells them?" (Romans 10:14). That is how you enter into life. You must first locate what God says, then believe it and act on it. This applies to healing as well. Take time to read and listen to the Word of God. Make discoveries and get fresh revelation on His desire for you to be healthy.

Beth's Testimony

After my wife gave birth to our first child, she suffered from postpartum depression. I knew nothing about postpartum depression. We were not expecting it. We were very excited to bring our first child home from the hospital. But shortly after getting home, my wife became depressed. She sat and cried. She felt hopeless, but didn't know why. Neither of us knew what to do. It was difficult to enjoy our new baby while my wife was constantly in tears. The doctors tried to help by medicating her. They put her on antidepressants, which didn't seem to help. Weeks passed, and finally, she slowly came out of the depression.

The same thing happened with our second child, but the depression was even worse this time. The hopelessness was more intense, and the depression lasted longer than the first time. It was horrible. What should be a joyful time in our household was anything but.

When we had baby number three, her postpartum was even more severe than the previous two times. With each child, she sank deeper and deeper into depression. She took the medicine the doctors prescribed, but it didn't seem to make a difference. This time the depression got so bad that I thought I might have to admit her somewhere. My wife couldn't function. She sat and rocked back and forth, pulling her own hair and crying. It was awful to see my wife that way. I was trying to comfort and care for her, along with a newborn baby and our two other little girls who wanted to know, "What's wrong with mommy?"

Once again, my wife gradually made her way back to being herself. Due to how extreme the third bout of depression was, we decided not to have any more children. We felt we couldn't go through something like that again. Our kids were getting older, and we didn't want them to see their mother in that state. With each child, the depression had worsened, and we didn't want to know what round four would look like.

A few years later, surprise! We found out my wife was pregnant again. But this time, we had learned some things regarding healing, and our faith had grown. We understood God's Word more clearly than we had before. My wife purposed to spend time listening to the Word of God. She listened to the Bible and anointed preaching almost around the clock. This time we understood that the Word of God is life to those who find it, and health to all of their flesh.

When the time came for the baby to be born, everything went smoothly. Instead of it being the fourth step down, deeper into the pit of depression, this time, there was no depression, not even a trace. We had saturated ourselves and filled our minds with the Word. We had preaching playing in the delivery room when the baby was born. We were determined to incline our ears to the Word, keep it in our hearts, and not let it depart from our eyes. We refused to be afflicted by the same thing that robbed our joy in the past. We understood that it was like medicine, and it proved to be exactly what it claimed, life and health.

God's Word will prove to be the same for you. But it starts with a commitment to His Word. Too many people in the Body of Christ have had their hearts and minds twisted by the enemy concerning the Word of God. People are willing to read anything in the morning. They will gladly read the back of a cereal box or the list of ingredients off the Pop-Tart box. But when it comes to reading the Bible, there is so much resistance to opening it up. Why? Because that is where life is found. That's where health is found.

The enemy will do everything to keep you from stepping into life. He will work to prevent you from stepping into health. Why? Because when you walk with a healthy body, it's a testimony of the finished work of Jesus. That's what Jesus said when He raised the paralytic off the mat. He said, "that you might know that the son of man has power to forgive sins, rise and walk" (Mark 2:10, 11).

People walking with healthy, strong bodies testify to the finished work of Jesus Christ, and the Devil doesn't want that truth on display. He comes to kill, steal and destroy, and one of his primary strategies is to keep you from the Word of God. But over and over and over again, you see healing comes from receiving the Word.

The Word Precedes Healing

But despite Jesus' instructions, the report of his power spread even faster, and vast crowds came to hear him preach and to be healed of their diseases.

— LUKE 5:15 (NLT)

When the crowds came to Jesus, they first heard Him preach. What followed *after* they heard the Word of God? Healing.

Luke 6:17 says there was a great multitude that, "came to hear Him and be healed of their diseases." Again, *first* they heard the Word, then healing followed.

This is the format Jesus gave us in the great commission. Jesus' instructions begin in Mark 16:15 with, "Go into all the world and preach the Gospel" and end in verse 18 with, "lay hands on the sick, and they will recover."

> And they went out and preached everywhere, the Lord
> working with them and confirming the word
> through the accompanying signs.
>
> — MARK 16:20 (NKJV)

They went out, they preached the Word of God, and God confirmed the Word with signs. The Word comes first. It starts with the Word, and the signs follow.

> "My people are destroyed for lack of knowledge."
>
> — HOSEA 4:6 (NKJV)

The Bible tells us in Galatians 3 that we have been redeemed from the curse of the law. Most Christians will say things like, "Yes, I've been redeemed. Hallelujah, I've been redeemed!" But if ever asked, "redeemed from what?" they are unsure. There is something very specific that you have been redeemed from, the curse of the law.

If you take the time to read Deuteronomy Chapter 28, you will learn exactly what the "curse of the law" is. If you have accepted Jesus, you have been redeemed from spiritual death. You have been redeemed from poverty. You have also been redeemed from sickness and disease. Without knowing the Word, you would know none of those liberating truths.

You must know the Word so you can walk in it.

There have been studies done where scientists took fleas and put them in a little glass dish. The fleas could jump right out of the glass dish and go do whatever fleas do. But the scientists then put a glass lid on the dish. The fleas would jump up and hit the glass lid. After repeatedly hitting the lid, the fleas eventually gave up. The experimenters then removed the lid so the fleas could go free. But because the fleas did not know they'd been set free, they stayed in that glass dish and starved to death.

They could have been off jumping around, chewing on a dog or people's ankles or whatever fleas like to spend their time doing.

Instead, they died. Why? *Lack of knowledge.*

That ridiculous flea experiment is very similar to what happens to Christians who don't know what the Word of God has to say. They don't know about all God has accomplished on their behalf. Why? They have not "found" it or discovered it in the Word.

Over and over, we see that the Word comes first. Jesus said, "You will know the truth, and the truth will set you free" (John 8:32). What comes before freedom? Knowing the truth.

> The people who know their God shall be strong and
> carry out great exploits.
>
> — DANIEL 11:32B (NKJV)

Where does being strong and doing great exploits start? With knowing their God.

How do we come to know God? Through His Word.

If you need healing, God's Word has what you need. But maybe you are reading this, and your body is healthy and strong. There is an important application for you as well. Paying close attention to the Word is not just something to do when you get a bad report from the doctor. *It is a lifestyle.* We are to walk daily with our "ear inclined" to God's Word, never letting it depart from our eyes. There is something available to us that is even better than getting healed—never needing to be healed.

If you have read the book of Exodus, you know about some of the extraordinary ways God cared for His people. While the children of Israel were in the wilderness, God performed all kinds of amazing miracles. When they were hungry, He gave them manna. When they wanted something besides manna, He brought them quail.

When they needed water, and there wasn't any readily available, God performed miracles to get them water. They drank water that came out of a rock on more than one occasion. An old filthy swamp that no one could drink from was miraculously changed into fresh, sweet water in Exodus 15.

But when they got into the promised land, no more manna appeared each morning. No more quail were offering themselves up for dinner when they opened the front door of their houses. There was no more water coming from rocks. Something had changed. Now they had their own wells to draw water from. In fact, the Bible says they had wells that someone else dug for them (Deuteronomy 6:11). In the Promised Land, they had good rich soil to plant crops in and grow whatever they wanted. They had land to raise herds of animals and could eat their own fattened calves.

Which was better?

Life in the wilderness or life in the Promised Land?

The Promise Land was better.

That is where they wanted to be all along. But once they were there, they were responsible for getting up and tilling the ground. They no longer saw the miracles of provision they saw in the wilderness, but they had something even better. *God had blessed them with the ability to live without needing those miracles.*

Something very similar is true for us. Miracles of healing are fantastic. We believe in them, and they are wonderful. But it is also a miracle to walk in divine health and not need to be healed. God has blessed us with the ability to live our lives with healthy, strong bodies. Again, I am in no way trying to diminish miraculous healings. It is great to need a miracle and receive it. Even better, though, is to never get to a point where you need healing because you are walking in divine health.

Keeping our eyes on the Word is not something we do when we require a touch in our bodies, but to experience the health God has made available every day. God's Word is not a place to visit like a hospital; it's a place to live.

> My Son, give attention to my words; Incline your ear to my sayings. Do not let them depart from your eyes; Keep them in the midst of your heart; For they are life to those who find them, And health to all their flesh.
>
> — PROVERBS 4:20-22 (NKJV)

God's Word is a Sword

The Word of God is not just bread. The Bible says the Word of God is sharper than any two-edged sword. So as you take time to read the Word of God, it is like a scalpel going to work. It can cut away every whisper of the mind telling you, "You know what? Your case is unique. Other people can acquire healing, and it's pretty much true for them, but not you. You're just going to suffer with that condition. That's just going to be the way it is. In fact, it's only downhill from here. It's going to get progressively worse..."

The enemy will work to convince you that somehow you are exempt or excluded from this bread. Anything along those lines is a lie from the enemy.

The Word of God can draw a dividing line and cut that garbage out of your life, leaving what is true. You need the Word of God to slice those things away and to divide lies from truth properly.

Jesus said, "You will know the truth..." But not just know it. He said that it will do something in your life. In John 8:32 He said, "You will know the truth and the truth will set you free." Think about that for a minute.

You will know the truth and the truth will set you free.

The truth is liberating. The truth takes a yoke off of your shoulders and sets you free. When a doctor tells someone, "Your condition is getting worse" there is no liberation. It does not bring them freedom when someone is told that they have diabetes, cancer, the flu, or whatever. It brings bondage.

If it does not set you free, then what do you know? You know it is not the truth, because Jesus said, "You will know the truth, and the truth will set you free." Refuse to accept sickness or diagnoses that rob you of freedom. They are lies!

If it's not liberating, if it doesn't set you free, then it is not truth. Too many people have been subjected to lies that they consider the truth. They live according to information that falls short of being truth. You'll know the truth, and the truth will set you free. You must learn how to differentiate.

Allow the Word of God to divide between joint and marrow, between the thoughts and intentions of your heart (Hebrews 4:12).

Let God's Word show you what is true and what you don't have to accept. Learn how to apply this litmus test to whatever emotions, thoughts, or whispers come into your mind. A distinguishing characteristic of truth is that it liberates. You know if it is truth or not by whether it sets you free or puts you under a yoke of bondage.

CHAPTER 6
BASE LEVEL PROVISION

When Jesus referred to healing as the children's bread in Matthew 15, He made a wealth of revelation available to us. He could have used any analogy, but He intentionally selected bread. He could have said, "It's not right to take the children's special family heirloom" or "It's not right to take their prized possession. It's not right to take their treasure." He didn't say any of those things.

He equated healing with the children's bread. We have said healing is not supposed to be rare and hard to come by. It should not be something that just a few people get to experience. It is base level provision for the Children of God, and we must understand it as that.

Jesus also said, "It is not good (right, proper) to take the children's bread away from them." Anything that tries to take your healing from you, whether it be poor doctrine, bad teaching, or a bad attitude, according to Jesus, violates what is right.

Jesus didn't say, "You know what? It's good, every once in a while, for someone to suffer with a condition because they can learn a few things and become more Christ-like." He didn't say, "It reveals or builds character." He said categorically, "It is not good, not right, not proper to take the children's bread because it has been paid for and belongs to them." Healing is the children's bread. It is base level provision for anyone who is a child of God.

Another thing that keeps people from receiving healing is when they learn to enjoy the sympathy that comes along with their condition. Growing up, we teased my brother because he seemed to enjoy being injured or having some form of sickness. He liked it because he enjoyed the attention he got. One time he hurt his neck while playing on a slip-n-slide in our neighbor's backyard. He laid there on the ground until a group of neighborhood parents came out to check on him. Once a small crowd had assembled, he managed to pull himself up to his feet and begin limping home.

When my daughters were younger, they loved to wear Band-Aids; not necessarily because they needed them, but for decoration. When we were out somewhere people would see one of my little girls wearing a bunch of Band-Aids and ask something like, "Oh, what happened? Did you hurt yourself?" "She's fine," I would explain. "She just likes wearing Band-Aids because it gets her attention." Some people handle any kind of illness the same way. When they get a diagnosis or begin to feel symptoms, they don't fight it; they actually embrace it because of the attention they receive. They love the way their condition makes them "special."

I am not anti-sympathy or compassion, but it is a mistake to fall in love with the attention or sympathy that sickness brings. Don't fall in love with your ability to complain about how bad you have it because you become like Esau. You trade away your birthright, the children's bread, for a bowl of soup. You trade a healthy, strong body for sympathy and sad comments, "Aw, poor him, poor her." People's sympathy isn't that good anyhow. It is not worth it.

Do not limit how special you are by how sick you are or how bad you have it. You carry the likeness of Jesus Christ; that's what sets you apart and makes you unique. Don't be special because you can only eat certain things, or else your allergies flare up. Don't let that determine how special you feel. In doing so, you trade away the blessing God has for you and what He's provided for you through the sacrifice of Jesus. Healing is the children's bread. He wants you to have it. He has provided it for you.

We have already mentioned one of the primary things keeping people from receiving their healing is they are not certain if it is God's will for them to be healed or not. Most people will say, "I know God *can* heal me. I know He's all-powerful. God can do anything." But when they pray for healing, they pray, "God, *IF* it is Your will ..." That type of prayer undermines the faith necessary to acquire healing.

One way that we can answer questions regarding God's will to heal is to look at what God has provided in Jesus.

Provision Has Been Made

My kids might not know if it is my will for them to have ice cream. Maybe I do, maybe I don't. They can wonder about it and debate among themselves. But if I load them up in the car, take them to the best ice cream shop in town, march them up to the counter, let them place their order, slap the money down on the counter, and smile as the waitress slides a big bowl of ice cream in front of them, at that point, my will for them regarding ice cream could not be more clear.

It would be shameful for them to still say, "Boy, I don't know if Dad wants us to have ice cream or not." I've already paid for it. I made the purchase specifically for them to enjoy it. It is a matter of whether they will claim it and savor it or stand there wondering about my will while it melts.

This applies to healing. A simple and clear answer whether healing is God's will for us is found by looking at the Word of God and seeing that provision is already made. If we see that healing is part of God's provision for His children, the question of His will is answered. If we see healing is paid for it becomes easy for us to claim it.

> Who Himself bore our sins in His own body on the
> tree, that we, having died to sins, might live for
> righteousness—by whose stripes you were healed.
>
> — 1 PETER 2:24 (NKJV)

This verse talks about Jesus. It lets us know He carried our sins. He carried them or bore them in His body. It talks about when He went to the cross. Our sins came on Him while on that tree. Now, why did Jesus bother carrying our sins? This verse tells us exactly why, "That we, having died to sins, might live for righteousness."

The reason Jesus carried our sins was so we could be righteous. Jesus carried our sins for one reason, so we could be clean. He carried them so we could be free and have sin completely removed from our lives, making us righteous. In fact, the last verse of Second Corinthians chapter five says Jesus *became sin*. Why? So we could *become the righteousness of God* in Him.

Based on these verses, we can go to God and receive forgiveness. The reason God forgives is not just because He is a kind, loving, and patient God. A very real price was paid to acquire forgiveness. Hebrews 9:22 says, "Without the shedding of blood, there is no forgiveness of sins." Without shedding blood there is NO forgiveness of sins. This means, apart from the sacrifice of Jesus, if you sinned and came to God and worked up your best apology speech with just the right amount of tears, God *could not* forgive you. If you said, "God I am so sorry. I'll never do it again, I promise." God could say, "Boy, I feel bad about it. I'm glad you realized what you did was wrong," but what He could NOT say is, "You are forgiven." Blood must be shed.

God's forgiveness is not based on His kind personality or the mood you catch Him in. It is based on a provision that has already been made; blood was shed on your behalf. When we know there is forgiveness in Jesus based on His provision, we can receive forgiveness by faith.

> If we confess our sins, He is faithful and just to forgive us our sins and to cleanse us from all unrighteousness. If we say that we have not sinned, we make Him a liar, and His word is not in us.
>
> — 1 JOHN 1:9, 10 (NKJV)

We make Him a "liar" if we say we have not sinned—because we have "all sinned and fallen short of the glory of God" (Romans 3:23). But this passage tells us if we come to God and confess our sins, He is faithful. He is faithful, not just to forgive our sins but to also cleanse us from all unrighteousness.

1 John 1:9 is a wonderful verse; one I have clung to many times. At times I've made mistakes and knew that I blew it. I felt terrible and dirty and full of remorse. So, I went to the Lord and confessed my sins, "Lord, I know I messed up. I know I shouldn't have done it. Please forgive me." I confessed my sin, but I still felt guilty and ashamed, like a big dirt ball that God wanted nothing to do with. I felt like I couldn't really worship God, as if I was excluded from His presence.

Maybe you have been in a similar situation. It is in times like this when 1 John 1:9 has been so important to me. Because of the truth of that verse, I was able to say, "I know I feel this way; I feel guilty, unforgiven and dirty. But the Bible tells me if I confess, He is faithful. He is faithful to forgive me. He is faithful to cleanse me." I could hold on to that truth and know I was clean and forgiven, despite how I *felt*. In the next couple of verses, John goes on to write this:

> My little children, these things I write to you, so that
> you may not sin. And if anyone sins, we have an
> Advocate with the Father, Jesus Christ the right-
> eous. And He Himself is the propitiation for our
> sins, and not for ours only, but also for the whole
> world.
>
> — 1 JOHN 2:1, 2 (NKJV)

He, Himself was the propitiation; that means He was the sacrifice. He took our place. He paid the price. We know God is faithful to forgive our sins, but *why?* His ability and faithfulness to forgive and cleanse is directly linked to Jesus being the propitiation. It also says that Jesus is our advocate with the Father. In that role, Jesus doesn't just say, "Father, You really need to forgive them. They are super-duper sorry." No, that is not where forgiveness comes from. Jesus was the propitiation or sacrifice. He *personally* paid the price of sin in our place. The one who carried our sins stands before the Father as a constant witness that the price has been paid in full.

You can know, that you know, that you know you are forgiven. You don't have to go to God and say, "God, I'm really sorry. If it's Your will, could I please be forgiven? God, I'd like to be righteous and clean, but I'm not sure where You stand on it. I don't know if You want me right-eous or clean."

You never have to pray that way.

You know that He wants you clean and that He forgives you. How do you know?

Because He paid for it.

I know this is basic, but I am laying a foundation for us to take the next step. Going back to 1 Peter 2:24, after telling us Jesus bore our sins on the cross, or on that tree, so we could be righteous, He then includes "by His stripes you were healed." In doing so, he is linking the forgiveness of sins so we can be righteous, with the cleansing of our bodies so that we can be healthy. He makes this connection because the provision comes from the same source; Jesus' atoning work. The same work that provided forgiveness of sins and salvation also made provision for the healing of our bodies. If it is the same work that supplied it, it has the same availability for anyone who believes.

Most Christians have a similar understanding of Romans 10:13, "Everyone who calls on the name of the Lord will be saved." Salvation is available in ample supply.

You see in the Great Commission that the availability is limitless; proclaim the Good News to *every creature*. Jesus' work on the cross has made salvation available to *all*. If salvation and healing both come from the same source, then they have the same level of "supply." If they both have the same supply, then one cannot be limited while the other is unlimited. Healing, like salvation, is in abundant supply.

Just like you know it is God's will to forgive based on provision, you can have the same confidence regarding healing. It is not about catching God in the right mood. It is not about being one of the lucky ones. It is not jumping through all the right hoops. It is about the provision God made through Jesus. Healing has already been provided. It is the children's bread.

> Surely He has borne our sicknesses and carried our
> pains; yet we esteemed Him stricken, smitten by
> God, and afflicted. But He was wounded for our
> transgressions, He was bruised for our iniquities,
> the chastisement of our peace was upon Him and
> by His stripes we are healed.
>
> — ISAIAH 53:4, 5 (NKJV)

In 1 Peter 2:24, Peter quotes from Isaiah 53:4, saying, "Surely, He has borne our sicknesses..." If your bible says griefs, hopefully, it has a little number with a footnote. You can look down at the footnote and see the real meaning of the word.

In Hebrew, it is not "griefs." It is "sicknesses." So literally, it says, "Surely, He has borne our *sicknesses.*" That is the same language Peter used regarding our sin. Jesus carried them, or "He has borne our sins."

Why did He carry our sins? So that we can be righteous. Then why did He also carry our sickness?

Jesus carried our sins so we could be completely free from sin and have sin removed from our lives as far as the East is from the West. Why did He carry our sicknesses? For the same reason.

By His stripes, by the beating He took on His flesh, healing was made available for you and me. Just like we are told, "Jesus became sin," Isaiah tells us Jesus *became* sick.

> And Jehovah hath delighted to bruise Him, He hath made Him sick.
>
> — ISAIAH 53:10 (YLT)

Why did God the Father delight in making Jesus sick? Did He receive some warped enjoyment seeing Jesus suffer? No. God knew by Jesus becoming sick, He was providing healing for you, and He delights in your healing.

Healing is the children's bread. You know it is His will because He paid for you to have it. But just because something has been purchased for you doesn't mean you automatically get to enjoy it.

I was recently in line at the grocery store waiting to make my purchase. There was a gentleman in front of me who put his items on the little conveyor belt, made his purchase and then walked out of the store. I stepped up to the register, ready to buy my items, but as I did, the cashier realized the man who had just made his purchase had left all of his groceries behind. He paid for everything and then walked out of the store.

The cashier called to another employee and had them get the man's groceries and take them to him in the parking lot. Those groceries had been paid for and rightfully belonged to that man. But unless he grabbed ahold of them, he would have returned home without what was his. It is the same with you and healing. It has been provided, but you still need to grab hold and claim it for yourself.

The Devil is a liar (John 8). He is also a thief (John 10). What does a thief do? A thief doesn't take things that belong to him. A thief, by definition, takes things that belong to somebody else. Healing is yours, but that doesn't mean the Devil won't come and try to take it from you. As a thief, that is exactly what he does.

Don't go by other people's experiences or even your own past experience, "Well, you say healing has been provided, but I've suffered a lot of sickness. How do you explain that? You say healing is ours, but my uncle loved the Lord and still died of cancer."

Understand that people get robbed. People get lied to and stolen from. But that does not have to be your case. You can choose to grab hold of what belongs to you and demand the provision become a reality in your life. Choose to defend what is yours. Just because something is yours, doesn't mean you get to enjoy it without effort. You have to stake your claim and defend it from the thief.

In Acts chapter 22, the apostle Paul was in Jerusalem preaching the gospel. He had an audience of people listening as he told them Jesus is the Messiah. But when he told them the Good News was also for the Gentiles, the crowd suddenly turned on him. They began to riot and wanted to kill Paul.

And they listened to him until this word, and then they
raised their voices and said, "Away with such a
fellow from the earth, for he is not fit to live!"
Then, as they cried out and tore off their clothes
and threw dust into the air, the commander
ordered him to be brought into the barracks, and
said that he should be examined under scourging,
so that he might know why they shouted so against
him.

— ACTS 22:22–24 (NKJV)

When the Roman officers saw a riot was taking place, they brought
Paul inside to be "examined." They planned to beat him until they got
the truth out of him.

And as they bound him with thongs, Paul said to the
centurion who stood by, "Is it lawful for you to
scourge a man who is a Roman, and uncon-
demned?" When the centurion heard that, he went
and told the commander, saying, "Take care what
you do, for this man is a Roman." Then the
commander came and said to him, "Tell me, are
you a Roman?" He said, "Yes." The commander
answered, "With a large sum I obtained this citizenship." And Paul said, "But I was born a citizen."
Then immediately those who were about to
examine him withdrew from him; and the
commander was also afraid after he found out that
he was a Roman, and because he had bound him.

— ACTS 22:25–29 (NKJV)

Paul was bound, and the Roman soldiers were about to scourge him. Roman scourging was not a few swats on the rear end to discipline someone. They were about to lay his back open with a violent beating. That is what the Romans did. They delighted in beating people and showing dominance. But Paul had rights and privileges because of his citizenship. He had certain rights that corresponded with how and where he was born. But unless he spoke up and claimed those rights, he would have received that physical abuse just like someone without any rights.

Those privileges would not do him any good unless he claimed them. Only when he spoke up and said, "Hey, hold on a second. It's not lawful to treat someone, born the way I was born, in this way." Otherwise, he would have received the beating.

That is what happens to many believers.

The privilege of health and healing has been provided. If you are a child of God, it belongs to you. You're a citizen of Heaven. Because of your second birth, healing is your bread. Paul would have been beaten unless he spoke up and demanded his rights.

You have to stand on the Word of God and claim your rights as a citizen of His Kingdom. You will suffer sickness and disease and everything everyone else must suffer until you open your mouth and say, "These are my rights as a child of God I insist on them being realized in my life. Everything that is contrary to that is a lie from the enemy, and I refuse to be stolen from."

The enemy will abuse you physically if you allow it. The enemy will steal your health.

If I broke into your house tonight and stole your TV, you wouldn't get up in the morning, see wires hanging where the TV was and say, "Oh. I guess that wasn't my TV after all." Would you? You would say, "Where is *my* TV? That was *my* television. Where is it?" You know it rightfully belongs to you. But too often, when believers are robbed of divine health they respond with an attitude that says, "Oh, I guess it wasn't my health anyway."

The enemy will try to deceive you. You will be lied to. He will try to convince you that you can't be healthy because sickness is just natural, or it's hereditary, or God is using it to teach you, or some other lie. Don't believe it. It is your health. It has been provided. Healing is the children's bread!

CHAPTER 7
HEALING IN COMMUNION

For I received from the Lord that which I also delivered
to you: that the Lord Jesus on the same night in
which He was betrayed took bread; and when He
had given thanks, He broke it and said, "Take, eat;
this is My body which is broken for you; do this in
remembrance of Me." In the same manner He also
took the cup after supper, saying, "This cup is the
new covenant in My blood. This do, as often as you
drink it, in remembrance of Me." For as often as
you eat this bread and drink this cup, you proclaim
the Lord's death till He comes.

— 1 CORINTHIANS 11:23-26 (NKJV)

Y ou have the right, as a child of God and citizen of His Kingdom,
to be healthy; but you must *claim* your right.

When you receive communion, it is a celebration of what has been
accomplished on your behalf. Jesus said to do it in remembrance of
Him. There are a couple of ways that you can remember something.

You can remember something, and it is simply recollecting or reminiscing, recalling a memory. For example, if I said, "Remember graduating from high school?" or, "Remember dropping out of high school?" (whichever the case may be). You could say, "Oh, yeah! I remember that." As you remember, you may recollect some specific details of the event, your cap and gown, the commencement ceremony, etc. But there is another way you can remember something that is not just recalling information in your mind. When you remember something this second way, it changes your focus and behavior.

Once, I was sitting at my desk working when I suddenly *remembered* I had a meeting scheduled and was supposed to be somewhere else. When I *remembered*, I sprung up from my seat, grabbed my keys, and hurried to my car because I knew I was running late.

When I *remembered*, it changed what I was doing. It changed where I was going and what the rest of my day would look like. That is the kind of remembering talked about in 1 Corinthians 11.

If I asked my wife, "Hey, do you remember when we got married?" she could respond, "Oh, yeah, I remember." We could then remember it together, recalling how that day went. Maybe even look through a photo album remarking, "Yeah, I remember that day. Remember what the weather was like? You looked so nice..."

We can remember it that way, or we could remember it in the second way. My wife could ask, "Remember when we got married?" And I could respond, "Yes, I remember. I don't just remember what we were wearing or what the cake looked like. I remember standing in front of you and making my vows. I meant them with all my heart. I remember putting this ring on and knowing I was being marked with a covenant till death do us part. I meant it then, and I mean it now." I could remember it in a way that I'm calling myself back to that same dedication. I could call myself back in alignment with that commitment and stir up the same resolve and fortitude. That is the way we are told to remember. Not just remember what Jesus did, as in, "Oh, yeah, that was nice. Now that you mention it, I do remember the story. He carried the cross up a hill and stuff." That is not the kind of remembrance we are called to. We are to remember what has been provided and call our lives back into alignment.

Jesus said, "This do in remembrance." He was instructing us to make sure we are in line with His provision. We aren't being asked to just recollect, "Can anyone remember if Jesus died or not?"

"Yes, He did."

"Okay. Mission accomplished," and we move on.

No. What did Jesus purchase on our behalf?

Am I living like that? Am I walking in righteousness? Am I free from sin? Am I free from sickness and disease?

If not, I need to *remember* what Jesus accomplished for me. I need to *remember* in a way that *moves* me to take whatever action necessary to get lined up with that reality. But it's more than just remembering, Paul continues,

> Therefore whoever eats this bread or drinks this cup of
> the Lord in an unworthy manner will be guilty of
> the body and blood of the Lord. But let a man
> examine himself, and so let him eat of the bread
> and drink of the cup. For he who eats and drinks in
> an unworthy manner eats and drinks judgment to
> himself, not discerning the Lord's body.
>
> — 1 CORINTHIANS 11:27–29 (NKJV)

In verse 29, it mentions receiving communion in an "unworthy manner." This is not talking about unworthy people, referring to people who have sinned. We have all sinned. That is precisely why this sacrifice was made.

Unworthy people are why Jesus established a new covenant. Our sinfulness is why Jesus bore our sins on the cross. Don't eliminate yourself from receiving communion because of this statement. That isn't what is referred to here. It doesn't say "whoever is unworthy"; it says whoever does this in an "unworthy manner."

The "unworthy manner" is not properly appreciating the significance of what we are handling in the communion meal. We see this more clearly as he continues.

> For this reason many are weak and sick among you, and
> many sleep.
>
> — 1 CORINTHIANS 11:30 (NKJV)

"For this reason." What reason? The reason is what he just mentioned in verse 29. They were "Not properly discerning the Lord's body." In the communion meal, the Body of Christ is the bread. Because people had not properly discerned the Body of the Lord, he says, "many are weak and sick among you, and many sleep."

In the natural, the things he lists are common. People growing weak, getting sick, and people dying are expected. It is considered a regular part of life. But these typical, expected things are pointed out as inappropriate for the children of God. This is not how the people of God are supposed to be living. The things most people accept as normal are given as "red flags" to let Christians know something is off.

Paul was telling the church, when it comes to these "naturally occurring things," you should not be living like everyone else. There was something available to them that they were not properly accessing.

They were failing to discern something, and that failure was causing them to live at the level of people who don't know the Lord.

What weren't they discerning? They were not properly appreciating the bread in the communion meal. They were receiving in an unworthy manner, and because of that, they were subject to growing weak, growing sick, people dying before their time. People were passing away before they had accomplished everything God planned for them.

Why Bother with the Bread?

In the Old Testament, there are foreshadows, or types, of the communion meal. When it comes to the bread, we see repeatedly that it communicates healing and divine health. At the last supper, when Jesus passed around the cup, He said it was His blood which was shed "for the forgiveness of sins" (Matthew 26:28). He also said His blood was the New Covenant (Luke 22:20).

When it comes to salvation, Jesus' blood pretty much has everything wrapped up, providing both the forgiveness of sins and a New Covenant with God. Salvation is certainly worth celebrating and acknowledging. If that's all there is in the communion meal and sacrifice of Jesus, it would be plenty. But if that *is* all there is, then why do we waste our time with that little wafer and talk about the Body of Jesus? We might as well go straight for the juice and forget about the bread. But the bread bears tremendous significance as well.

The Bible says, "by His stripes you are healed" (Isaiah 53:5). Where were Jesus' stripes? They were on His flesh...His body. It is specifically through what happened to His flesh that healing was provided. When Jesus passed the bread to His disciples, He said, "This is My body," or My flesh, "broken for you."

Another place we see this is in the Passover meal. Again, the Passover meal was a type, or a foreshadow, of the communion meal. The

Israelites were instructed to take the blood of the Passover lamb and put it on the doorposts of their homes (Exodus 12). Doing this protected them from the death angel and spared their lives. That was a picture of the salvation we have by the blood of Jesus. But after telling them what to do with the blood, the Lord gave them further instructions on what to do with the "flesh" of the Passover lamb.

He did not say, "You know what? I hadn't really thought about the rest of the lamb. All I really wanted was the blood. You guys can make sandwiches with the flesh or do whatever." No, very specific instructions were given on how to eat the flesh of the Passover lamb.

They ate it with a belt around their waist and with their walking stick in their hand. They ate it "in haste" and with sandals on their feet. Why? Because they were anticipating a change of situation. They were ready to travel and leave the place where they were.

After they ate this meal, the Bible says the Lord, "brought them out with silver and gold and there was none feeble among His tribes" (Psalm 105:37). The Israelites plundered the Egyptians and left loaded down, carrying away Egypt's gold and silver (Exodus 12:36). God brought His people out wealthy.

When the Israelites left Egypt, they were not leaving a place where they had been treated pleasantly. When they began their journey, they were not coming out of years of rest and relaxation. They hadn't been receiving spa treatments during their time in Egypt. They were slaves, and they were treated brutally.

> So the Egyptians worked the people of Israel without
> mercy. They made their lives bitter, forcing them to
> mix mortar and make bricks and do all the work in
> the fields. They were ruthless in all their demands.
>
> — EXODUS 1:13, 14 (NLT)

They were worked hard and malnourished. When Moses showed up, their conditions went from bad to worse (Exodus 5:7). They had been beaten, worked tirelessly, and deprived of things you and I take for granted. That is the way they lived their lives. There were open sores and injuries to back. There were wounds from being whipped and crushed limbs from working with large bricks. Slaves are never a picture of health. People were sick, injured, and crippled. But something happened to them before they began their exodus from Egypt. Psalm 105:37 says that when God brought them out of Egypt, "there was not one feeble among their tribes."

Experts believe three million Israelites left Egypt. Three million people with ZERO sick among them! After 400 years of brutal treatment, three million Israelites walked out of Egypt, and there was not *one* weak or sick person. Young or old, it didn't matter; there was not one single feeble among them. Not only were they healthy enough to set out on a journey, but they also had to be strong and healthy enough to carry all the Egyptian's gold and silver. They had to have strong backs to make that journey, carrying all their own possessions plus the things they had plundered.

What happened? What changed them from beaten-down slaves to strong and able-bodied men and women, ready to make a great journey? We know the blood of the lamb had protected them from the death angel, but then they ate the lamb's flesh. When they ate that lamb, they did not just receive the natural strength that a belly full of food provides. They received supernatural strength from the flesh of the lamb, and the flesh of that lamb is a foreshadowing of the bread in the communion meal.

When the Israelites were in the wilderness, what did they eat for 40 years? They ate manna. In John 6, Jesus identifies Himself as a fulfillment of the manna. He said, "Your fathers ate manna while they were in the wilderness, but I am the true bread that comes down from heaven" (John 6:43-51).

Immediately after identifying Himself as a fulfillment of the manna, He begins talking about eating His flesh and drinking His blood (John 6:53-58).

> And the children of Israel ate manna forty years, until they came to an inhabited land; they ate manna until they came to the border of the land of Canaan.
>
> — EXODUS 16:35 (NKJV)

For 40 years, they woke up in the morning, opened the tent and there was manna. Day after day, month after month, year after year, manna, manna, manna. But something else happened over those 40 years as they continued to enjoy their "daily bread."

> Your garments did not wear out on you, nor did your foot swell these forty years.
>
> — DEUTERONOMY 8:34 (NKJV)

For 40 years, they traveled through the wilderness carrying everything they owned and the precious metals of the Egyptians. They carried it over brutal terrain in the heat of the desert. During that time, they didn't suffer so much as a swollen foot.

I know people who can't spend an afternoon at an amusement park without their ankles looking like cantaloupes by the end of the day. This verse is not just talking about feet. It depicts how *entirely* healthy they were. With all that traveling, all the walking in brutal temperatures, everything they were carrying, among millions of people, you couldn't find so much as a swollen foot. That is supernatural health!

How did they achieve this level of health in their body?

Every day they ate their daily bread as they received manna, and Jesus said, "That was good, but I am a fulfillment of it, and you must eat my flesh and drink my blood."

I am trying to establish and build our faith in the significance of the bread in the communion meal. In all these types of bread in the Old Testament, we see supernatural health and strength. Let's look at another example in the life of Elijah.

> Then he lay down and slept under the broom tree. But as he was sleeping, an angel touched him and told him, "Get up and eat!" He looked around and there beside his head was some bread baked on hot stones and a jar of water! So he ate and drank and lay down again.
> Then the angel of the Lord came again and touched him and said, "Get up and eat some more, or the journey ahead will be too much for you."
> So he got up and ate and drank, and the food gave him enough strength to travel forty days and forty nights to Mount Sinai, the mountain of God.
>
> — 1 KINGS 19:5–8 (NLT)

Elijah received food from Heaven that gave him strength to travel for 40 days AND nights. What was the food? It was bread provided from Heaven. That food did not just give him spiritual strength. When he ate it, he received strength in his physical body to hike and walk through the day and the night, day after day, until he reached his destination. He traveled for 40 days and 40 nights straight! He was on a mission, up and down over mountains until he came to the place God wanted him to be and finally decided, "I'll spend the night here."

There was something supernatural in that bread that gave him strength. That kind of strength is not something a natural meal can provide. When you receive communion, you can receive supernatural strength. But many people make the mistake that Elijah did. The first time Elijah received the bread, he was not fully engaged. He didn't realize how significant it was or what it would accomplish in his body. He ate it and went back to sleep, behaving as if the bread had only done what natural bread could. The angel had to wake him up again and say, "Elijah, this is serious. This isn't just a snack. This is a supernatural meal; you need what this bread can do for you." He was, in a sense, acting like the Corinthian church and not properly discerning the bread.

God desires for you to have "daily bread." Jesus instructed us to pray that way, "Give us today our daily bread." That prayer for bread is not just a request for spiritual nourishment. Yes, God wants you nourished spiritually, which is certainly part of it. Our daily bread includes understanding and revelation as we feed on the Word of God. Our daily bread includes receiving the mind of Christ, divine direction, a fresh filling of the Holy Spirit, and other spiritual provisions. But God is not just concerned with spiritual things.

If Jesus' ministry in the Gospel accounts represent the heart of the Father—and they do—then God clearly cares about the physical, everyday aspects of our lives. In Matthew 15, Jesus ministered to a large crowd of people on a hillside, preaching and teaching for three days. What did he do before he sent them away? They were being taught by THE teacher, Jesus Himself.

For three days, Jesus poured into them. They were receiving rich spiritual nourishment. But as Jesus got ready to send the crowd home, He didn't say, "You guys are loaded with spiritual food. You've been eating like kings! Now go home, and thanks for coming." No, He said, "Wait, hold on. I'm not sending these people anywhere until we get a good meal in their bellies. I don't want them weak on the way home. I don't want them to stumble and fall. I don't want them to faint. I want them to be physically strong, healthy, and able to make the journey."

Don't over-spiritualize the "daily bread" we are to request in the Lord's Prayer. Obviously, the spiritual is the more important, but Jesus did not neglect the physical. He cared about people's bodies so much that He performed awe-inspiring miracles to provide lunch.

When Jesus reveals that God wants us to receive "daily bread," we understand that He wants us supplied daily with what is needed to keep our bodies running healthy and strong. We are to receive daily bread, and that bread communicates divine health.

In 2 Kings 4, a group of men are about to enjoy a pot of stew together. While preparing the stew, one man goes out to collect some ingredients. Somehow, as he is collecting wild gourds and herbs, he also manages to collect something poisonous. They sliced up the ingredients he collected and put them in the pot. When it was finally ready, they began to eat. As they started eating it, they realized they were eating poison and cried out, "There's death in the pot. This stew is poisonous!" How did Elijah respond? He didn't kick the pot over and say, "I sure am glad I didn't have any of that." He didn't put a Mr. Yuck sticker on the pot's side and say, "All right, this is off-limits."

What did he do? He said, "Bring me some flour," and he put it in the pot (2 Kings 4:41). After adding flour, the stew was no longer poisonous, and the men went ahead and ate the rest of it. Not only did the flour change the stew from poisonous to non-poisonous, it changed the men who had already consumed the poison. They went from poisoned men about to die to healthy men enjoying some soup. No natural flour or bread eradicates poison and works as an antidote. That flour is another picture of the bread in the communion meal, and its ability to bring health and life.

As you eat the communion bread, it does some eating too. It devours every germ and every disease. It consumes every virus and everything that tries to afflict your body and swallows it up with the strength of Jesus Christ Himself. But we must come to the communion meal in faith, believing.

The Corinthians had no problem approaching the communion table and eating. They were doing that regularly. But they were *not* doing it worthily. They were not properly discerning and appreciating the Body of Christ. So even though they were eating communion all the time, they were missing out on the benefits of communion. Don't allow the communion meal to simply be a religious experience.

In the Old Testament, whenever God provided some kind of bread in a covenant meal or by a supernatural provision, the people who ate it experienced a manifestation of supernatural health and strength. That bread, or meal, did something miraculous in their physical bodies that would not have happened otherwise. Those Old Testament examples are types of communion meals.

In the Bible, every time there is a type and then a fulfillment of the type, the fulfillment is always greater than the type. The foreshadowing symbol is never greater than what it is foreshadowing. If there is healing and strength in the type, you can be sure it is also available in the fulfillment.

In Luke 24, Jesus appeared to men on the road to Emmaus, but they didn't recognize Him. When they arrived, they sat down to eat a meal together. Jesus took some bread, broke it, and blessed it. As He did this, it says the eyes of those men came open, and they recognized Jesus (Luke 24:31).

The breaking of that bread is another picture of communion. As they received the bread, it also brought a revelation of Jesus. The same thing happens when people experience the healing God has provided; it reveals who Jesus is.

In Luke 5, a paralyzed man was brought to Jesus on a mat. Jesus told the man that his sins were forgiven. The Pharisees and other religious leaders thought this was blasphemy, so Jesus provided a revelation of who He was. How? He said, "So that you may know that the son of man has authority on earth to forgive sins," then he turned to the paralyzed man and said, "rise and walk" (Luke 5:24). The Pharisees had said, "only God can forgive sins" (Luke 5:21), and they were right. Jesus' healing of this man was a revelation of His identity. When you receive healing or walk in divine health, it is a revelation of the reality of Jesus and who He is. One of the ways it is ministered is through the communion bread.

Healing in the 23rd Psalm

The 23rd Psalm is messianic in the sense that it talks about the ministry of Jesus as our shepherd. Jesus identified Himself as "the good shepherd" in John 10. Psalm 23:5 tells us that this shepherd "prepares a table before me." What table did the good shepherd prepare for us? The answer is the Communion table.

Some say this "table" refers to the wedding feast when we get to Heaven. We will eat a feast with Jesus in Heaven. But that is not what this is referring to. We come to this table "in the presence of our enemies." Our enemies won't be present when we eat with Jesus in Heaven. Another way we know this is found in verse 6. It tells us that one of the benefits of this table is, "Surely, goodness and mercy will follow me all the days of my life." It talks about something the shepherd has provided to be a blessing to us in this life, not just someday when we get to Heaven. In fact, you can see a progression in these verses.

> You prepare a table before me in the presence of my enemies; You anoint my head with oil; My cup runs over. Surely goodness and mercy shall follow me all the days of my life; And I will dwell in the house of the Lord Forever.
>
> — PSALM 23:5,6 (NKJV)

"You prepare a table before me." That table is the communion table. What are the elements of the communion table? The body and blood of Jesus, or the atoning work of Jesus. After people enjoy this table, what happens next in the 23rd Psalm? "He anoints my head with oil." That is a picture of the Holy Spirit poured out on us. Notice how the progression of the 23rd Psalm parallels the believer's experience. Only after Jesus finished His work on the cross and returned to Heaven could He send the gift of the Holy Spirit. Only after coming to know Jesus—enjoying the atonement—can a believer receive the baptism of the Holy Spirit. In the 23rd Psalm, what happens after one enjoys the table and the anointing? "Surely goodness and mercy will follow me all the days of my life" (Psalm 23:6a).

Goodness and mercy are two specific benefits that come to someone after they enjoy what is provided at the table. On this communion table, there is bread and wine, or Jesus' flesh and blood. As we have established, the blood speaks of forgiveness of sins. That is the mercy of God.

Under the Law, on the Day of Atonement, the priest took the blood of the sin offering and sprinkled it on the mercy seat. The blood of Jesus allows us to enjoy the mercy of God. Because of His blood, we get to go into the presence of God, where otherwise, we have no business being.

The mercy of God allows us to be clean and have fellowship with God Himself. We can approach Him with boldness and confidence because of His mercy. But it is not only mercy that follows a person enjoying this table, there is also goodness.

The mercy correlates with the blood of Jesus, or the drink. The *goodness* of God comes from the bread, the broken body of Jesus. The blood of Jesus allows us to enjoy spiritual benefits; the body of Jesus provides physical benefits. That is the goodness of God. God is so overwhelmingly good, He has not just saved our souls but also made provision for our physical bodies. Because of what happened to Jesus' flesh, healing is ours. "By His stripes, we are healed" (Isaiah 53:5).

God's mercy and goodness can be accessed by this table that our shepherd has provided for us. Surely goodness and mercy will follow you all the days of your life!

Healing is undoubtedly a significant part of God's goodness. Still, ongoing health and financial provision are also included in this goodness. The bread in the communion meal communicates the provision God made available through Jesus in the physical realm. The blood of Jesus communicates the provision made in the spiritual realm.

When you look at a person—as long as everything is ok—you cannot see their blood. Their blood is in an "unseen realm," so to speak. In the same way, the provision in the "unseen realm" or the spirit realm, is imparted to us by the blood of Jesus; forgiveness of sins, freedom from bondage, spiritual life, anointing, etc.

What you *can* see when you look at someone is their flesh. Their flesh is in the "seen realm." The flesh of Jesus imparts to us the provision made available in the "seen" or physical realm. When we see Jesus' substitutionary work for us, we can determine if it is in the physical or spiritual realm. Jesus became sick so we could become healthy (Isaiah 53). Jesus became poor so we could become rich (2 Corinthians 8:9). These are examples of provision made by Jesus in the physical realm. An example of spiritual provision is that Jesus became sin so we could become the righteousness of God (2 Corinthians 5:21).

When you prepare to receive communion, set in your heart that you are about to receive something more than the world's smallest snack portion. What do you need? As you approach the body and blood of Jesus, be like the woman with the issue of blood. She said in her heart, "I know if I can just touch the hem of His garment, I will be made well." Many people came in contact with Jesus that day, but she was different.

She knew exactly what she wanted and made contact deliberately. "If I can just touch His clothes, I know this bleeding that has plagued me for 12 years will dry up immediately. My body's going to be strong." She didn't say, "I hope if I can touch Him, something nice will happen. I think something good will probably come about as a result of it." She had purposed in her heart and set her faith, "I know this is what I'm after. Here's what I'm believing for. Here's what I'm putting a draw on."

If she could acquire that impartation by brushing up against His clothing, how much more is available to us by receiving the broken body of Jesus and the shed blood of Jesus?

When you receive the communion meal, you are accessing the provision of God. All that Jesus suffered and died to provide to you is available. It is His goodness and mercy represented by his flesh and blood. Set your faith to receive what you need every time you contact the communion table.

CHAPTER 8

THE FATHER'S PROVISION ON DISPLAY

B efore we begin talking about healing as "showbread" allow me to review.

We started in Matthew chapter 15 with the story of a woman who came to Jesus and asked for healing for her daughter. Because she was not a Jew, Jesus said, "it is not good (not right, not proper) to take the children's bread and give it to the dogs." In this analogy, He was not talking about a real dog, He was talking about Gentiles, particularly this woman and her daughter.

In this analogy, the dogs represent people. And when He mentioned "bread," He was not talking about actual bread, He was referring to healing. That is where we learn the concept of healing being the children's bread. We've reviewed this several times, but it is important for us to get it settled and rooted in our hearts. Too often, we think of healing as something that rarely happens or is hard to come by.

You have heard stories of miraculous healings that happened far away overseas or some time long ago in the olden days. For many people, that is the only place healing happens, in old stories. The problem is, when you believe healing is something rare, something that hardly ever happens and is hard to come by, then that's exactly what it becomes in your life. It is rare, hardly ever happens, and is hard to come by.

God sees healing as common, not rare. He calls it the children's bread. That is Jesus' perspective on healing; it is base level provision for the children of God. If you saw a dad giving their child a slice of Wonder Bread, you wouldn't say, "My goodness, that is father-of-the-year material right there. He needs to be careful. He will end up spoiling his kid with that excessive treatment."

If you saw a parent give their child a piece of bread, you wouldn't think you had witnessed anything special. You wouldn't think much of it at all.

Again, Jesus could have used any analogy He wanted. He could have chosen something rare. He could have said, "Healing is the children's once-in-a-lifetime trip to Disney World," but He intentionally compares it to something common.

Even in today's culture, bread is *extremely* common. At restaurants, it is not unusual to have loaves of bread placed on your table for you to eat before they bring you the food that you order from the menu. Their *business* is selling food. That is how they make their money. All other food you have to order specifically and pay for. But bread...you can just have it.

Every once in a while, I take my kids to feed ducks at a local park. Sometimes when we arrive, someone else has beaten us to it. On more than one occasion, we have arrived to find bread lying all over the ground on the bank of the river. When we show up with our bags of bread, the ducks seem to roll their eyes in disgust as if to say, "Are you serious? More bread? Can't you see it lying all over the ground? Enough with the bread!"

Bread is common. Jesus intentionally compares healing for children of God to something commonplace. There must be a shift in your heart, your way of thinking, and in your faith. When you believe for healing, you're not shooting for the stars and stretching God to His limits. You're simply accepting what He considers basic provision for you as His child.

Healings and miracles were common in the early church.

> Now God worked unusual miracles at the hands of
> Paul.
>
> — ACTS 19:11 (NKJV)

The next verse tells how handkerchiefs or aprons that Paul had touched were taken and put on sick people and they were healed. Verse 11 calls those healings "unusual". The word translated "unusual" literally means "not the ordinary."

If miracles were happening that needed to be classified as "not the ordinary," what does that tell us? It lets us know that a level of miracle in the early church was considered commonplace or ordinary.

Miracles/healing had become so common that they needed to identify some of them as "not the ordinary." I am not trying to diminish the significance of healing. I'm trying to build faith that healing is very obtainable because of God's goodness and provision. The more God's healing power is on display, the more His goodness is on display.

Bread On Display

In the Old Testament, God gave instructions for building both the Tabernacle and the Temple. He gave very specific details about how things were supposed to look, what all should be inside, and how it was supposed to be arranged. As God gave instructions about His house, one of the things He gave details about was a table, the Table of the Presence. That table was supposed to be set up in the Holy Place.

Tables are significant in the Bible. A table in the Bible represents fellowship, communion, people gathering together for a meal, and enjoying a relationship with one another.

When we look at the furnishing of the Tabernacle and Temple, we can see the desire in the heart of the Father that eventually led Him to create a new and better covenant. He wanted His people with Him, in His presence. He desired fellowship. That is what a table represents. An example of this is found in 1 Corinthians 5.

In 1 Corinthians 5, Paul talks about people who call themselves believers but are still walking in sexual immorality. These people said they followed Jesus but were unwilling to get rid of sin in their lives. Paul instructed the Corinthian church to not even eat with those people. Why did he say not to eat with them? Does it have to do with the danger of consuming a hamburger at the same time as someone else? No. It isn't about digesting food. He is talking about close fellowship with those people. Close fellowship is what a table represents.

God instructed that there was to be a table called the Table of the Presence in the Holy Place. It was set up in the presence of God with 12 loaves of bread on it, one for each of the tribes of Israel. The bread on the table was called the showbread.

Way back in the days of the Tabernacle and the Temple, God wanted His provision for His people to be something that was put on display. They called it the showbread. God desired, and still desires, His provision for His people to be something that is shown. There is a very important parallel between that showbread and the bread of healing that we have been discussing. The bread represented God's provision for His people, and it was to be kept on display on the Table of the Presence.

Healing is the Showbread

Healing is the children's bread, and in a very real way, healing is also the showbread. Healing puts the provision of God on display in people's lives. It gives evidence or testimony to His provision. People who experience God's healing power can testify about God's provision. It is like the showbread being put on display. Healing is God's provision and His care for His people. That is what was happening throughout Jesus' ministry as He healed people.

> Then great multitudes came to Him, having with them the lame, blind, mute, maimed, and many others; and they laid them down at Jesus' feet, and He healed them. So the multitude marveled when they saw the mute speaking, the maimed made whole, the lame walking, and the blind seeing; and they glorified the God of Israel.
>
> — MATTHEW 15:30, 31 (NKJV)

People brought multitudes of sick people, laid them down at Jesus' feet, and He began to heal them. People were marveling. They were astonished. They saw people walking who could not walk before. They watched as people who could not talk before opened their mouths and began talking and singing praises to God. People who were paralyzed got up and started moving around. As they witnessed these miracles, the healing provision of God, what did they do in response? It says they began to glorify God. Why? Because it was a manifestation of God's provision for His children. His care for them was on display.

People were excitedly pumping their fists and saying, "Boy, my knees feel great! I haven't felt this great in years! Thank you Lord! Only You are this good to me!"

They lifted their voices and glorified God. Why? Because healing was like the showbread on the Table of the Presence. In the presence of God, there is rich provision for the children of God.

As you read through God's Word, anytime He gets involved in provision, there is always an abundance. There are no stories of God providing, and people barely squeak by. It is always above and beyond. When Jesus multiplied the loaves and fish, do you think God knew how much would be needed to satisfy the bellies of that multitude? Of course He did. He could have provided the exact amount, down to the last crumb. But instead, the disciples spent the afternoon picking up 12 baskets full of "more than enough."

In Luke 5, Jesus told Peter to take his boats back out fishing. Peter's men had spent all night fishing and caught zero fish. It would have been a testimony for those men to have caught just a few dozen fish. God knew that catching anything on their first cast after what they had experienced the night before would be a sign. He knew the exact number of fish those nets could hold without tearing and how many fish those boats could hold without taking on water. His nature to go above and beyond trumped His concern for the nets. Peter and his men caught so many fish that the nets tore, and the boats began to sink. When God gets involved in provision, there is overflow and abundance, and healing is no exception.

Let's look at more examples of healing as showbread. In Luke 5, a group of men let down a paralyzed man through the ceiling of a house. The man is lowered on a mat in front of Jesus. After pronouncing that the man had been forgiven of his sins, Jesus said, "So that you may know the Son of Man has authority to forgive sins." He then turns to the paralyzed man and says, "Get up, take your mat, and go home." The man returned home carrying the very mat that had been carrying him. It was a manifestation of the provision of God. In Jesus, there is both healing and forgiveness of sins. Jesus was putting the provision of God on display. It was showbread.

In John chapter three, Nicodemus came to Jesus to ask Him questions. In John 3:2, he said, "Rabbi, we know that You are a teacher come from God." How did Nicodemus come to that conclusion? How did he know that Jesus came from God? Jesus could have been a deceiver, a false prophet, or any number of things. How did Nicodemus *know*? "Rabbi, we know that You are a teacher come from God; for no one can do the signs that You do unless God is with him" (John 3:2). It was the signs, the healings, the things that were taking place in Jesus' ministry. Those things were proof. They were putting on display that Jesus had come from God. It was God's provision for His children.

As Paul traveled and presented the Gospel to Gentiles, he said that something specific convinced the people he preached to his message was real.

> They were convinced by the power of miraculous signs
> and wonders and by the power of God's Spirit. In
> this way, I have fully presented the Good News of
> Christ from Jerusalem all the way to Illyricum.
>
> — ROMANS 15:19 (NLT)

What caused these Gentiles to give their lives to Jesus was not just a superior-sounding philosophy. It was not just talking about God's character. There were manifestations. There were signs and wonders and the moving of God's Spirit. They were seeing the power of God. They were enjoying the showbread.

Paul said, "In this way," referring to signs and wonders, "I have fully presented the good news of Christ." Meaning that if there was no "showbread," then it was an incomplete presentation of the good news. A full presentation of God's provision and goodness *must* include signs, wonders, and healing. Healing is the children's bread. It is an essential part of the Gospel, and if missing, it is an incomplete presentation of the good news. Healing is like showbread; it puts the provision of God, the care of God, the power of God, and the love of God on display so people can see it.

God's goodness and His provision are not supposed to be limited to theoretical and ethereal talk, "Somewhere out there in the spiritual realm, God has some power, or so I've heard..." It's not supposed to be that way. That is what Jesus' ministry was all about; taking spiritual realities and causing them to affect things in the natural. That is exactly what Jesus' arrival was in the first place. It was spiritual impacting the natural.

The Spiritual Impacting the Natural

In John 1:1 it says, "In the beginning was the Word, the Word was with God, and the Word was God." In verse 14, talking about Jesus taking on flesh, it says, "And the Word became flesh and dwelt among us..." In those verses, we are told that the "Word was God." In John 4:24, Jesus said, "God is Spirit." Jesus' arrival was the spiritual realm invading the physical realm.

That does not just describe Jesus' birth, but His entire ministry. He took spiritual realities and imposed them on the physical realm. He took on flesh but walked according to the spirit. He used the reality of the power of God to supersede the "realities" of the physical realm.

When Jesus multiplied the bread and loaves, that was not natural. According to the natural realm, you cannot use a few fish and loaves to feed thousands of people. We know the portion sizes were not microscopic, allowing for the mass distribution, because we are told the people "Ate their fill." After they finished eating, there were baskets of leftovers. In the natural, you can't have more at the end than you had at the beginning. Jesus did not limit Himself to what was possible in the natural but invaded the natural/physical with the power of God.

This is what takes place with healings. Leprosy is not a condition that just suddenly clears up. It was a serious condition that was the equivalent of a long, slow death sentence. When Jesus healed someone of leprosy and made them whole again, He literally invaded their physical condition and enforced a supernatural reality on the situation.

Death is another condition that, naturally speaking, is not something people typically recover from, especially if you have a bad case of it like Lazarus did. But Jesus stood outside of Lazarus' tomb and cried out with a loud voice, and Lazarus came walking out. These are things that DO NOT happen naturally. Jesus was not walking according to the natural, He was walking according to the spiritual power and provision of God. Again, He was invading and impacting the physical realm with spiritual realities. But that was not just something Jesus did and then went away. Those were not things He did so we could talk about it. He was giving us an example to follow.

Jesus handed off the responsibility of invading the kingdom of darkness and the natural realm with the Kingdom of God to the Body of Christ. The showbread on display in the Tabernacle, the Temple and in the ministry of Jesus is still on display today. The Church should continue putting showbread, God's provision, on display in people's lives. In the house of God, there should still be showbread. In the days of the Tabernacle and Temple, the showbread was not just a loaf of bread they made once and left lying on that table forever. It was supposed to be made fresh regularly. Every week they were to have fresh bread. It is the same thing with healing. God still desires His provision for His children to be fresh.

Thank God for testimonies that happened years ago. I love to read about miracles in the Word of God and stories from great men of God like Smith Wigglesworth, John G. Lake, and Kenneth Hagin. I praise God for those testimonies! But testimonies of God's mighty works should not all be 50-plus years old. We need fresh bread to put God's provision on display *now*.

If the power and provision of God only *used* to be available, then there is a staleness to our testimony. We also need some stories of our own. We need people willing to step out in faith and bake some fresh show-bread to display God's provision, power, and healing now. We need it manifest and on display today in people's lives. God desires His show-bread to be on display to be fresh. It is a revelation that healing is the children's bread, and it is still available.

> "And these signs will follow those who believe: In My
> name they will cast out demons; they will speak
> with new tongues; they will take up serpents; and if
> they drink anything deadly, it will by no means
> hurt them; they will lay hands on the sick, and they
> will recover."
>
> — MARK 16:17, 18 (NKJV)

Jesus said there will be people who lay hands on the sick, and those sick people will stop being sick. He said this is a sign that accompanies or follows a certain kind of person. What category of people should lay hands on the sick and see them recover? He doesn't say, "These signs will accompany people in full-time ministry positions, apostles and tele-evangelists," or, "These signs will accompany the fivefold ministry." No. He said, "These signs will follow those who believe." Any level of Christian, walking in faith, should be operating on this level. When someone is sick, there should be a testimony following shortly. "They will lay hands on the sick, and the sick will recover."

> Now, Lord, look on their threats, and grant to Your
> servants that with all boldness they may speak Your
> word, by stretching out Your hand to heal, and that
> signs and wonders may be done through the name
> of Your holy Servant Jesus.

> — ACTS 4:29, 30 (NKJV)

This prayer in the early church is not being prayed only for people in leadership positions. They were praying for anyone who considered themself a servant of God. They prayed, "grant to Your servants." And what were they asking that the servants would be granted? "That with all boldness they may speak Your Word." This is important. How do they define "speaking Your Word"? "By stretching out Your hand to heal." He equates speaking the Word of God, or preaching the Good News, with healings taking place.

Again, "grant to Your servants that with all boldness they may speak Your Word."

How is the Word of God declared?

"By stretching out Your hand to heal, so signs and wonders may be done through the name of Your holy Servant Jesus." They understood the importance of having fresh showbread to accompany the Good News.

When they prayed this prayer, do you know what happened next?

> And when they had prayed, the place where they were
> assembled together was shaken; they were all filled
> with the Holy Spirit, and they spoke the word of
> God with boldness.

> — ACTS 4:31 (NKJV)

They prayed for healing and miracles, and the building started to shake. Why did it start to shake? Was God frustrated with them for focusing on miracles? Do you think He wanted to startle them a little because He was aggravated that they focused on people getting healed? Maybe the building shook to show God's rage as if to ask, "How dare you ask for healings and miracles?!?! Who do you people think you are?!?!"

No. It showed He was shaking with excitement. God had some people He could work with. They were saying, "Lord, we want our heart to line up with Your heart. We want to do what You've called us to do."

At the end of verse 31, you can see God immediately answered their prayer, "and they spoke the Word of God with boldness." You can also see He answered that prayer as you read through the book of Acts and see signs and wonders, miracles and healing. That is how we are supposed to operate as the Body of Christ.

If someone had no knowledge of Christianity or the Church and sat down to read the New Testament, they would get the impression that people who follow Jesus should be walking in signs and wonders and lay their hands on the sick and see them recover. If you knew nothing else and had no religious teaching, and just sat down to read the Gospels and the book of Acts, you would come to the same conclusion. You would come to that conclusion because that is what the Bible says will be the case. There are claims made about the Body of Christ in the Word of God, and the Body of Christ needs to position itself to make good on those claims.

A person who promises a gift but doesn't give it is like
clouds and wind that bring no rain.

— PROVERBS 25:14 (NLT)

This verse is about someone who says they have something good to bring but never actually delivers it. That person is like a cloud that just goes by, not doing anyone any good even though they claim they can bless someone. They say, "There is a gift for them, a promise they can claim, a power they can experience, relief they can have," but that person never gets to enjoy what they are being told about. A person who makes empty claims about God's provision is just like a cloud that makes it appear as though it will release much-needed rain, but it never delivers.

2 Peter 2:17 says, "These men are as useless as dried-up springs of water, promising much and delivering nothing." Some people are like dried-up springs of water. They promise much, but they don't deliver what they promise.

Years ago, I went backpacking on the Appalachian Trail with a friend. It was a hot, dry August, and foolishly, we didn't pack enough water. We assumed we could get water from streams along our hike, but we never encountered any. In fact, we completely ran out of water and went an entire day hiking in the heat with absolutely nothing to drink. We were getting desperate. We didn't know what to do. The region was experiencing a drought that year, so many of the streams had entirely dried up. We looked at our map and found a place 5 miles farther down the trail where there was a spring. At that point, even though we did not feel like hiking another 5 miles, we decided that was what we needed to do.

It was hot, we were exhausted, and we had already gone more than a day without water. After another long hike, we finally saw the little trail marker indicating that the spring was just ahead. We were so excited we started to run. We ran down the little side trail to where the spring was supposed to be, but when we got there, it was dry. We were so desperate for relief from our thirst that we slumped to the ground, staring at the dry spring. There is a profound level of disappointment when you think you're about to receive refreshment—when you think you're about to receive what you need—and then don't. It said on the map that *this* was the spot where the water was located! It said on the little sign along the trail that *this* is where water could be found! I was overcome with disappointment and discouragement to get there and find that it didn't really have what it claimed to offer.

People should never experience those feelings when they come to the Body of Christ. When they read in the Word what the people of God are called to do and be, and they look to the Church for relief, they should not find that we are dried-up springs. We should not be people who promise much but only deliver disappointment. When the Church promises much but delivers nothing, it causes problems. There are two ways to eliminate these problems.

If your problem is promising much and delivering nothing, one of the ways you can solve it is by simply not promising anything. You could promise nothing and then make good on your claims by delivering nothing. Many churches have taken this approach. They explain away the Word of God and why its promises are no longer for today. To avoid discomfort, they lower the Word of God to the point that it promises nothing; that's exactly what their people experience —nothing.

Promising nothing is one way to protect people from disappointment. Personally, I do not like that option. I am not comfortable coming up with explanations about why the Word of God does not work anymore and why the promises of God were for other people and not for us. I cannot bring myself to tell people that God's Word is not valid. Thankfully, there is another option.

The other option is to promise and deliver much; to make good on what the Word of God has to say. We can be people who are *not dried-up* springs, but people with rivers of living water flowing from them!

You can be the person God destined you to be, a person filled with the Spirit of God! When people come to you, they won't find disappointment; they will find that God keeps His Word. You will be a person who puts the provision of God on display. Healing is the children's bread. There is an incredible parallel between that bread of healing and the showbread. God is a good provider, and He wants provision on display in your life, family, and church. God wants fresh showbread on display.

As you read through the Old Testament, types of Christ are seen. Certain people like Joseph, Moses, and David were types of Christ. The Passover lamb and Jacob's ladder were types of Christ. Types of Christ are not supposed to be limited to the Old Testament. Types of Christ in the New Covenant are not objects or animals; they are men and women who have accepted Jesus. That is why Paul said, "It is no longer I who live, but Christ lives in me" in Galatians 2:20.

In this New Covenant, we are *all* supposed to be types of Christ; filled with His Spirit and carrying out His will. According to Colossians 1:27, that is the mystery of the Gospel, "Christ in you."

Previously we discussed communion and how the 23rd Psalm is messianic in that it describes Jesus. It tells us about the Lord being our shepherd. When Jesus came, He identified Himself as "the good shepherd" (John 10). Jesus arrived and said, "Listen, it's Me. I'm the Good Shepherd." The 23rd Psalm talks about that shepherd preparing a table before us in the presence of our enemies.

There is a progression in the 23rd Psalm. Jesus prepared a table for us, the communion table. He prepares a table before me in the presence of my enemies. What happens after that?

That table represents receiving the blood of Jesus and the broken body of Jesus. It is a picture of the communion meal and of entering into the New Covenant. The next verse says, "He honors me by anointing my head with oil. My cup overflows." After we enter the New Covenant, we are given a picture of being filled with the Holy Spirit. After someone receives Jesus, they can receive the anointing— the Holy Spirit.

Then it says, "And surely goodness and mercy will follow me all the days of my life." We talked about goodness and mercy representing the two elements in the communion meal. The mercy of God was made available through the blood of Jesus. His blood allows us to experience forgiveness, God's love, His graciousness, the new covenant, and the ability to come into the presence of God. It's the mercy of God. The bread in the communion meal links to the goodness of God. The bread is the broken body of Jesus, bringing provision for physical healing and material needs.

The idea of "goodness and mercy" following the believer directly connects with what Jesus said in Mark chapter 16. He said, "these signs will follow those who believe." What signs? Supernatural signs. God's goodness and His mercy; seeing people healed, seeing people delivered. That is what will follow those who believe.

In the 23rd Psalm, there is a progression: "You prepare a table"; a picture of the communion table/body and blood of Jesus' salvation. "You anoint my head with oil"; receiving the anointing of the Holy Spirit. "Surely your goodness and mercy will follow me"; signs and wonders accompany.

When someone experiences a healing that is showbread, their testimony is showbread. Somebody saying, "Listen, God touched me. He healed me. I used to have this condition, but thanks to Jesus, I don't have it anymore." That is showbread. That is the provision of God on display, taking the provision of God out of the spiritual realm and making it manifest in the physical realm. As Christians, that's the assignment we have. We're not supposed to just hang out. We've got a job to do. In fact, read what Jesus said in Matthew chapter five.

"You are the salt of the earth. But what good is salt if it has lost its flavor? Can you make it salty again? It will be thrown out and trampled underfoot as worthless."

— MATTHEW 5:13 (NLT)

We are the salt of the earth. Salt is not typically used for decoration. When you put salt on your food, it's not because you want to put little crystal sprinkles on it just to jazz it up. When they put salt on meat to preserve it, salt has a job; it is supposed to accomplish something. Salt effects a change of some sort wherever it is applied. It is supposed to DO something.

You add salt because you want it to accomplish something. But what did Jesus say about salt that isn't getting the job done? What about salt that isn't doing what salt is supposed to do? He said it is worthless or good for nothing. That kind of salt is thrown out and trampled under feet. This is a significant statement. Think about where you walked over the last week. You probably went to lots of different places. Maybe you walked across the parking lot, maybe you went to work, you went to your car, or you went to the grocery store.

How much attention did you pay to where you stepped? You knew you were walking across the parking lot or down a hallway, but you probably weren't taking careful notice of each place you set your foot. That's why you can sometimes step in, or step on, things and not realize it until later.

Maybe you have smelled an unpleasant smell and traced the source to the bottom of your shoe. You realized that you stepped in the spot where a dog had relieved itself, but you were unaware at the time. Or maybe you noticed your foot sticking a bit as you walked and realized you had stepped on someone's chewed gum. Why didn't you simply avoid stepping on those things? Because you don't pay close attention to what you step on.

People don't notice what they walk on. Jesus said, "You are supposed to be the salt of the earth. You have a job to do as the Body of Christ!" Jesus told us to take spiritual realities and invade the natural sense realm. For example, freedom is provided for us in the spiritual realm. The power of sin is broken. We are supposed to take this provision, invade the natural realm with it, and cause people to know and experience forgiveness and freedom from the bondage of sin. It is the same with healing. Healing is provided. It is not supposed to remain in the unseen realm. Believers are to grab hold of it and impact the physical realm so that provision can manifest.

Jesus told us what happens when salt doesn't do its job; it is trampled under feet. That means it gets overlooked and unnoticed. Salt that loses its saltiness gets walked on, and people don't even take note of it. You can see that happening in the Church.

When the Body of Christ doesn't do what it is called to do, we are like salt that has been thrown out and trampled under feet. This is why you can have a community with a church on every corner, yet the community is completely unaffected. There are men and women who have accepted Jesus and carry His Holy Spirit, but few, if any, can tell they are different from anybody else. Christians live unnoticed among non-Christians.

Why? They don't distinguish themselves from anyone because they are not doing their job. As a result, they are getting trampled underfoot, and what is trampled is not noticed.

The Body of Christ is not supposed to be treated casually. As you walk, typically, the only time you notice where you have stepped is when something goes wrong. You take notice when you trip over something or smell something unpleasant. When the church fails to be salty, it receives similar treatment. Attention is only paid when something goes wrong; a high-profile pastor has an affair, someone embezzles funds, a child is mistreated, or there's a scandal. This is when the media reports and people pay attention to the church. This is not the way it is supposed to be. The evidence that someone is not doing what they are supposed to be doing, according to Jesus, is when people brush us aside and trample us under their feet. However, as we operate in power, lay hands on the sick, and see them recover, people will notice not our failures but the goodness of God.

Jesus has called us to produce showbread.

CHAPTER 9
USE IT

A s we learn about healing, we must be careful to put what we have learned into practice. We want to be doers of the Word and not hearers only (James 1:22).

> Then He said to them, 'Take heed what you hear. With the same measure you use, it will be measured to you;"
>
> — MARK 4:24A (NKJV)

Passages like this one are often used in relation to financial giving. The teaching typically goes something like this: if you use a small, or stingy, measure in your giving, then that is how it will be measured back to you when it comes to receiving. If you use a large or generous measure, then that is how it will be measured back to you. That teaching is accurate, and the principle is repeated in several passages of scripture in regard to giving (Luke 6:38, 2 Corinthians 9:6).

But in Mark 4:24, the word "USE" is used differently. In context, Jesus is talking about revelation and understanding. He has just told the parable of the sower where the Word of God is sown like a seed. Jesus explained that the person who hears the Word, holds on to it, understands it, and applies it, is the person who brings forth a 30, 60, or 100-fold return.

Immediately after explaining the parable of the sower, Jesus talked about lighting a lamp. He said people don't light a lamp and put it under a basket. Instead, a light is placed on a stand for all to see. Jesus is still talking about the light, or revelation that comes from the Word of God. That is what precedes verse 24.

> Then He said to them, "Take heed what you hear. With the same measure you use, it will be measured to you;"
>
> — MARK 4:24A (NKJV)

The subject Jesus is dealing with here is revelation. When He says, "the measure that you use" He is referring to making *use* of the revelation you have received. Your *application* of the things you have learned, heard preached, or read from the Bible is "the measure you *use*." The measure you actually put into practice will be measured back to you.

Jesus continued:

> "And to you who hear, more will be given. For whoever has, to him more will be given; but whoever does not have, even what he has will be taken away from him."
>
> — MARK 4:24B–25 (NKJV)

God will give you more in proportion to how you use revelation. On the other hand, whoever does not apply what they have learned will lose what they do have. This gives us insight into how the church has become the way it is.

Much of the modern-day Church is weak at best regarding the subject of healing. Many Christians are ignorant about what God's Word says on this topic. It is a subject that some preachers/teachers don't talk about. Often what is said is so wishy-washy that it does no good. We have moved backward instead of forward in our understanding.

For centuries the church has known about healing. You can't read through the gospels and not see the healing ministry of Jesus. But at times, we have allowed healing to be merely theological or theoretical. People have failed to put their understanding into practice in daily life. Jesus said whoever does not *make use* of revelation, even what he has, will be taken away from him. That means God can reveal truths to a person with the intent that they make progress. If that person does not make an application, it results in them taking steps backward instead of forward.

We must be careful not to be in the class of people who have a level of understanding regarding healing but move further and further from where God wants us. For that not to happen, we must use the revelation we have. Jesus said as we use what we have, we will increase and gain more.

The Bible says to despise not small beginnings (Zechariah 4:10). However, that is not an excuse to stay small. Everything in the Kingdom of God grows.

Jesus used agricultural examples to explain how God's Kingdom works. He described how a plant starts off small, takes time to grow, and brings forth fruit as it reaches maturity. The same principles can be applied when it comes to people ministering healing. You have to start somewhere.

I am not saying it can't happen, but for most people, the first time they pray for someone, it won't be raising a person from the dead. Faith grows. Start somewhere and begin exercising your faith by applying the Word of God.

Many people accept colds, headaches, allergies, sinus infections, upset tummies, and other minor ailments. They think those things are a normal part of life and are expected. But Jesus provided healing for those types of issues in the same way he provided healing from life-threatening illnesses. Instead of tolerating less serious levels of sickness, use it as a training ground to build up your faith. Don't wait for a report that you or someone you love has stage 4 cancer to believe for healing.

Before David fought Goliath, he built a resume of victories over lesser opponents. Fighting Goliath was not the first battle he ever had. David established a pattern of victory fighting lions and bears when far less was on the line than the fate of his nation. Those past victories prepared him so he could just keep on doing what he had always done when he faced a highly trained giant. Build a similar pattern in your life, a pattern of taking on whatever opponent attacks your health. When you or someone around you is under attack, fight.

Don't accept your child having a cold or a fever. Use it as an opportunity to make use of your understanding regarding God's provision for your healing.

The Body of Christ must develop a reputation for being "Christ-like" in this area. When people have a problem and need healing, their first thought should not be to go to a doctor but to a Christian.

Make use of the understanding you have. In your workplace, in your neighborhood, with your family; pray for the sick. Anoint your children or spouse with oil if they don't feel well. Run to the children's bread instead of the medicine cabinet. Do it because whoever makes *use*, with the same measure they use, it will be measured back to them. You will grow, progress, and get stronger as you apply the Word of God.

AFTERWORD
WHAT IF YOU'RE NOT A CHILD
OF GOD?

Healing is the Children's bread, but what if you are not one of God's children?

Many people mistakenly think that we are all God's children. That is not true. We are all God's creation, but there is only one way someone can become a child of God. Concerning Jesus, the Bible says, "But to all who believed him and accepted him, he gave the right to become children of God." (John 1:12 NLT)

God has made a way for you to be adopted into His family and become His child. That way is by putting your faith in Jesus and accepting Him as your savior and as Lord of your life.

Jesus said, "I am the way, the truth, and the life. No one can come to the Father except through me." (John 14:6 NLT)

If you have never accepted Jesus and been adopted into God's family, it is critically important that you do. We all need a savior because we have all sinned and we all fall short (Romans 3:23). Because of our sin, we have earned death and eternal separation from God in hell (Romans 6:23). But God is so merciful, His love for you was so great and being separated from you was so unacceptable to Him, that He sent Jesus to pay for your sins I die in your place (John 3:16-17). If you will believe what the Bible says about Him, and accept Jesus as your savior you can become God's child and receive eternal life.

If you would like to accept Jesus and become a part of God's family, pray this prayer, and mean it:

> *Dear heavenly Father, I realize today that I have sinned, I have made mistakes, and I need a savior. I believe with all my heart that Jesus is that savior. I believe that He died on the cross for me. I believe He paid for my sins and that God raised Him from the dead. I accept Jesus as my Lord & Savior. Come into my heart Lord Jesus. Forgive me of all my sins. Make me clean. Make me new. Make me who You want me to be. Fill me with Your Holy Spirit. I will serve You all my life. In Jesus' name, amen.*

If you prayed that prayer from your heart, the Bible says that you are a brand new on the inside! You are forgiven, clean and on your way to heaven! Now, get plugged into a Bible believing church and continue to grow as a child of God.

For more resources to help you continue learning and growing, go to www.LukeBrugger.com.

HEALING CONFESSIONS
BASED ON SCRIPTURE

I am convinced and sure that He who began a good work in me will continue until the day of Jesus Christ, developing and perfecting and bringing it to full completion in me.

— PHILIPPIANS 1:6

You, Lord, have taken my griefs (sicknesses, weaknesses and distresses) and carried my sorrows and pains. You were wounded for my transgressions, bruised for my guilt and iniquities; the chastisement needed for my peace and well-being was upon You, Jesus, and by Your stripes I am healed and made whole.

— ISAIAH 53:4-5

The thief comes only to steal and kill and destroy. You came, Lord, that I may have and enjoy life, and have it in abundance (to the full, till it overflows.)

— JOHN 10:10

I gratefully praise You, Lord and do not forget all Your benefits. You forgive all my iniquities and heal all my diseases. You redeem my life from the pit and corruption. You beautify, dignify, and crown me with lovingkindness and tender mercy. You satisfy my mouth with good things, so my youth is renewed like the eagle's.

— PSALM 103:2-5

I attend to God's Word and submit to His sayings. I will keep them in my sight, and in the center of my heart. They are life to me, and healing to my whole body.

— PROVERBS 4:20-22

God has not given me a spirit of timidity and fear. He has given me a spirit of power and of love and of a calm and well-balanced mind, discipline and self-control.

— 2 TIMOTHY 1:7

Because I have made you, Lord, my refuge, and the
Most High my dwelling place, no evil shall befall
me, nor any plague or calamity come near my
house. Because I have set my love on You, Lord,
therefore You deliver me. You set me securely on
high, because I have known Your Name. I call upon
You, Lord, and You answer me. You, Father, are
with me in trouble. You deliver and honor me.
With long life You will satisfy me and show me
Your salvation.

— PSALM 91:9-10, 14-16

You give power to me when I am faint and weary. In
my weakness, You increase strength in me. I wait
for You [expect, look for, and hope in You] and
You renew my strength and power. I will lift up
with wings of strength and rise as an eagle. I shall
run and not be weary, I shall walk and not faint or
become tired.

— ISAIAH 40:29, 31

Healing belongs to me. I was healed by the stripes Jesus
bore. I'm not trying to get God to heal me. I've got
healing, because by His stripes I was healed.

— I PETER 2:24

Even though I have a physical body, I will not carry on
warfare according to the flesh, using mere human
weapons. The weapons of my warfare are not physical (weapons of flesh and blood), they are mighty

before God for the overthrow and destruction of strongholds. I refute arguments and theories and reasonings and every proud and lofty thing that sets itself up against the true knowledge of God; and I lead every thought and purpose away captive into the obedience of Christ.

— 2 CORINTHIANS 10:3-5

I will not fret or have anxiety about anything, but in every circumstance and in everything, by prayer and petition, with thanksgiving, continue to make my requests known to God. God's peace, which transcends all understanding, shall garrison and mount guard over my heart and mind in Christ Jesus.

— PHILIPPIANS 4:6-7

ABOUT THE AUTHOR

Luke Brugger is married to his best friend, Beth and the proud father of four daughters. He is the Lead Pastor of Centerbranch Church, a growing church in Bridgeport, WV, with a mission to connect people with the newness of life found only in Jesus Christ.

You can reach him through his website:

www.LukeBrugger.com

Printed in the USA
CPSIA information can be obtained
at www.ICGtesting.com
LVHW040720031023
759951LV00005B/11